David,

well done, you made it.....!

I guess we will have to do two of these together each year for the next 50......

if your handicap drops!

Love

Carolyn + John

27. xii. 01.

Gary Player's
TOP GOLF COURSES
of the WORLD

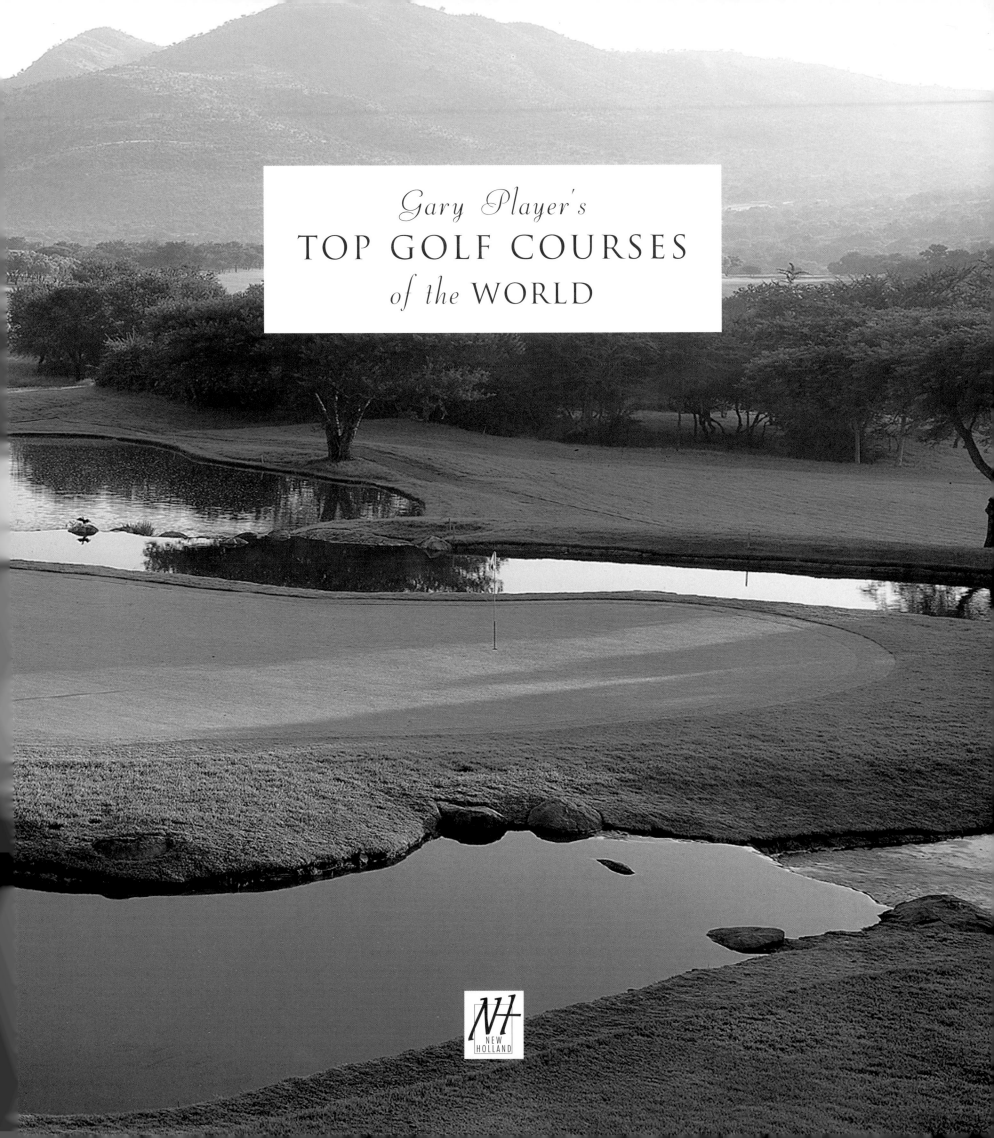

Gary Player's
TOP GOLF COURSES
of the WORLD

NH
NEW
HOLLAND

First published in 2001 by
New Holland Publishers
London • Cape Town • Sydney • Auckland

Garfield House
86 Edgware Road
London, W2 2EA

80 McKenzie Street
Cape Town 8001
South Africa

14 Aquatic Drive
Frenchs Forest, NSW 2086
Australia

218 Lake Road
Northcote, Auckland
New Zealand

ISBN 1 85974 5024

Designer: Geraldine Cupido
Commissioning Editor and Publisher: Mariëlle Renssen
Editor: Roxanne Reid
Illustrator: Steven Felmore
Picture Researcher: Sonya Meyer
Proofreader/Indexer: Ingrid Schneider
Consultant: Mark Rowlinson (UK)
Production: Myrna Collins

Reproduction by
Hirt & Carter (Pty) Ltd, Cape Town
Printed and bound in Singapore by
Tien Wah Press (Pte) Ltd
2 4 6 8 10 9 7 5 3 1

HALF TITLE: *A view across the 16th hole at the Turnberry Golf Club, Ayrshire, Scotland.*

FULL TITLE: *The Gary Player Country Club at Sun City in South Africa, was designed in the late 1970s.*

THIS PAGE: *The majestic ocean sweep of Pebble Beach on California's Monterey Peninsula seen from the short 5th hole.*

CONTENTS

ABOVE: *Valderrama in Spain, designed in 1975 by Robert Trent Jones, hosted the 1997 Ryder Cup, which was won by the European team captained by Spaniard Seve Ballesteros.*

FOLLOWING PAGES: *The Links at Fancourt in South Africa's southern Cape, created by Gary Player, opened for play in November 2000. Inspired by the great links courses of Scotland and Ireland, it will host the President's Cup in 2002.*

PREFACE

Over the past five decades of my professional golfing career, I have been fortunate to visit, play and study many of the great golf courses of the world, and have tried to use this opportunity to apply these experiences in the design of over 150 golf courses worldwide.

It is therefore a great pleasure to be involved with a book that gives me a chance to describe my favourite golf courses. Some of these were created by the Gary Player Design Company, others hold special memories through tournament successes, while still others have left lasting impressions through their playability, traditions or sheer beauty and harmony with their surroundings.

We have incorporated into this book many of the great old links courses of Scotland, England and Ireland, plus a selection of more recent 'links-like' courses that 'borrow' elements of links layouts. We have included a wide variety of parkland-style courses, from classic layouts such as Augusta National to modern creations from such diverse locations as Europe, Asia and South Africa. We have also looked at the modern trend in resort courses and tournament-specific courses so prevalent in the USA, and have covered those most spectacular of layouts – the ocean courses, from layouts such as the famous Pebble Beach in California to the recently opened Ria Bintan in Indonesia. Modern earth-moving machinery has allowed the creation of golf courses in previously inaccessible locations, so we have included a selection of desert courses from locations like Egypt and the United Arab Emirates, the bushveld courses of South Africa, and one of Switzerland's scenic mountain courses.

Rankings and selections of golf courses always tend to attract debate and controversy. We have tried to incorporate here examples of all the different types of courses – old and new; traditional and modern; built in a wide variety of settings, styles and geographic locations – to show how truly international this wonderful game of golf has become.

Gary Player

ABOVE: *Azaleas in full bloom around the green of the par-five 13th hole at Augusta National, USA. The course was the brainchild of amateur golfer Bobby Jones, whose design philosophy aimed to provide a tough examination for the best players without demoralizing the social golfer.*

GOLF COURSES

The great architects

Since golf's early days some 500 years ago the game has experienced several periods of evolution. Evidence of how it has grown over the centuries can be seen in the advances in equipment, particularly in the manufacture of the golf ball and the driver; the move in tournament format from matchplay to strokeplay; and changes in the character and appearance of golf courses.

The art of golf course architecture – a term first coined by renowned golfer and golf course architect Charles Blair MacDonald – has undergone an evolution of its own. While early golf courses were created by nature rather than an architect's hand and players found their own way from tee to green without the course dictating their strategy, modern courses are laid out by men who charge huge fees for both course design and construction.

While the identity of the first person actually to decide how a particular golf hole should look is lost in the misty origins of the game, it is recorded that the first group of people to dabble in golf course design were the early professional golfers. The most prominent of these was Old Tom Morris, a multiple winner of the Open Championship who lived at St Andrews where he ran a golf shop and acted as both professional and greenkeeper. Morris had a hand in the design of a number of classic layouts in the UK, including Muirfield in Scotland, Westward Ho! in England and Royal County Down in Ireland, a course deemed by many to be the finest venue for links golf in the world.

Morris popularized a course layout style that featured each nine returning to the clubhouse in a loop, as opposed to the first nine going out and the second nine coming back. To this day Morris's strategic layout at Muirfield remains one of the game's miracles of design. He laid out the first nine to play clockwise and the second nine to play anti-clockwise, thus ensuring

that golfers experience the wind from every conceivable angle, and are thus tested to the full.

The 1920s were regarded as the golden age of golf course design and construction. It was during this period before the Great Depression that men such as Donald Ross, Alister Mackenzie, Harry Colt and AW Tillinghast produced some of their finest works.

Colt, the co-designer of Pine Valley in New Jersey, USA, led the revolution that saw golf course architecture move away from the notion that all but the perfectly struck shot should be penalized. He believed golf courses should test all shots in a player's arsenal, but that there was no need to severely punish all less-than-perfect shots.

Mackenzie, an English surgeon who served in the Boer War and World War I, created some of the game's most revered venues, including Royal Melbourne in Australia, Cypress Point and Augusta National in the USA, which he co-designed with Augusta National founder and legendary amateur golfer Bobby Jones. Together with contemporaries such as Tillinghast, whose designs include Winged Foot and Baltusrol, and Ross, who created Pinehurst No. 2 and many other great layouts, Colt and Mackenzie laid down the foundation of golf course architecture. The principles they established were so sound that they are still in use today, although in recent times there have been some changes to accommodate the need for multiple tees and irrigation systems.

Through the years after World War II, architects like Robert Trent Jones adhered diligently to the golden principles laid down by Colt and company. Others such as Tom Fazio, Pete Dye and professional golfers turned architects such as Jack Nicklaus, Gary Player, Arnold Palmer and Tom Weiskopf combined tried and tested design guidelines and principles with innovation, lifting golf course architecture to new heights with their spectacular creations.

ABOVE: *The legendary Old Tom Morris had a considerable influence on golf course design in the United Kingdom, building courses in England, Ireland and his native Scotland. Old Tom and his son Young Tom won four Open Championship titles each between 1861 and 1872.*

FOLLOWING PAGES: *Carnoustie on Scotland's east coast was designed in the mid-1800s by Allan Robertson and Old Tom Morris. The view from behind the 1st green shows the new hotel opened in July 1999 prior to the 128th Open Championship.*

LINKS GOLF COURSES

Shaped by the hand of nature

Games similar to golf – like 'kolf', played in Holland, and 'chole', played in Belgium – existed in medieval Europe, but it is generally accepted that golf as we know it today originated on the 'linksland' of Scotland's east coast.

Linksland originally referred to the strips of sandy coastal land formed when the sea receded after the ice age. Over centuries, fine grasses and gorse bushes covered these undulating areas. Not suitable for agriculture, they were generally used as 'common ground' by the residents of nearby towns. Once golf became popular, golfers also ventured onto the linksland for their games. Today the word 'links' refers to coastal golf courses on which nature has dictated design and layout.

Despite varying opinions as to what defines a 'true' links course, several specific characteristics are generally found, although not all of these 'conditions' are essential. Certainly, many fine links courses, including some that have hosted the Open Championship, do not have all of them. Links courses are usually close to the sea, exposed to coastal winds. Design is dictated by nature since almost all were laid out before the advent of earth-moving machinery and landscape architecture. The subsoil tends to be sandy, while layouts typically wind their way through, over and around dunes covered with grasses and gorse bushes. The first nine holes usually head out from the clubhouse or starting point, while the second nine come back towards it – hence the terms 'outward' and 'inward nines'.

In the early days, golfers played to the same holes going out and coming back, but this became increasingly dangerous as the game grew in popularity, so it was decided to cut separate holes for the inbound nine. As a result, two holes were cut on the same putting surface, and 'double greens' were born. These are still featured on some courses today and many modern architects deliberately build one or two on new layouts to recreate a classic feel. The most famous are those at the Old Course, St Andrews, which has no fewer than seven.

Most of the world's links courses are on the coast of the UK and Ireland, although fine examples in other parts of the world include Paraparaumu in New Zealand and Humewood in South Africa.

Golf on links courses is very different to playing on parkland, desert or mountain courses. 'Links golf' demands a wide range of shots because of the vagaries of the weather, the undulating terrain, the fine strains of grass usually found on links courses and the firmness of the soil. Approach shots often have to be run to the pin by way of 'bump and run' shots, while deep bunkers are constructed of stacked soil bricks. Some, known as pot bunkers, are extremely small. (Well-known golf writer Bernard Darwin once wrote of a pot bunker: 'It has just enough room for one angry man and his mashie!') Water hazards are scarce on links courses but, when present, usually take the form of burns that run off to the sea. The most famous is the Swilcan Burn that runs in front of the 1st green at St Andrews.

LINKS-LIKE COURSES

The exhilaration offered by links golf has led today's golf course architects to replicate the characteristics of links courses in their designs. As the game of golf mushroomed across the globe during the course of the early 19th century, Scottish golf course architects spread the influence of links golf by incorporating links-like features into courses like Shinnecock Hills in the USA and Royal Melbourne in Australia. Modern architects like South African Gary Player have also used classic links features in layouts like the USA's Raspberry Falls and, more recently, The Links at Fancourt in South Africa.

Although these 'links-like' courses are often situated inland, golfers playing over the undulating fairways that wind between towering dunes find it hard to believe they are not close to the sea and that the layout is the work, not of nature, but of men with bulldozers and earth-moving machinery.

ABOVE: *Portmarnock, in County Dublin, Ireland, shows the rolling, treeless landscape typical of links courses. Set on an exposed peninsula between the Baldoyle Estuary and the Irish Sea, the course is at the mercy of the vagaries of wind and weather.*

ABOVE: *Turnberry golf course is built on a stretch of classic linksland on Scotland's Ayrshire coast. The green is protected by typical deep pot bunkers in the style of those found on the earliest courses, which were shaped naturally by sheep sheltering from the icy coastal winds.*

ST ANDREWS

The home of golf

Golf has been played over the Old Course at St Andrews in Scotland for close on 450 years. While golf courses have spread and multiplied throughout the world since those early days, Mother Nature's creation on a windy peninsula jutting into the North Sea remains one of golf's true masterpieces. St Andrews is a mecca for golfing pilgrims, amateurs and professionals alike, and attracts thousands of visitors each year.

St Andrews is known as the home of golf, not only because of its long golfing history, but also because this barren piece of rolling scrub and heather, over which golf's pioneers first established the game, has evolved into one of the largest golfing complexes in Europe.

Today, the St Andrews Links Trust manages six golf courses, a 44-bay practice centre and a large and comfortable clubhouse. It is also home to the Royal & Ancient Golf Club of St Andrews (generally referred to as the R&A), which is recognized as the game's governing authority by all countries except the USA and Canada.

The term 'linksland' refers to the bleak and windswept strip of land 'linking' the ocean shore and the fertile farming regions further inland. Sheep grazed freely over these inhospitable areas of rolling dunes, grass and low bush, rubbing hollows – the forerunners of bunkers – into the side of the hummocks to seek shelter from the harsh sea winds. It was on this linksland that golf was first played at St Andrews, over courses shaped more by nature than by man.

In 1552, the burgh issued a charter giving Archbishop John Hamilton permission to establish a rabbit warren on the links at the town of St Andrews. The charter also confirmed the rights of the townspeople to play golf over the links – the piece of land today known as the Old Course.

Resembling a billhook when seen from the air, the shape of the course has not changed over the centuries, but its original 22 holes were reduced to 18 in 1764. This was one of the first changes brought in by the Royal & Ancient, which at that time had only been in existence for 10 years, but it was influential to the extent that 18 remains the

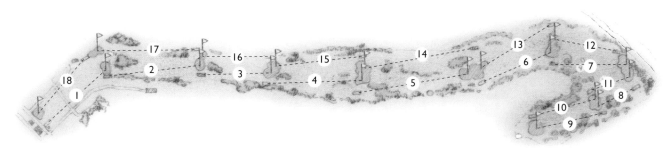

LEFT: *One of the most famous views in golf: the bridge over the Swilcan Burn leading to the 18th hole of the Old Course at St Andrews, with the Royal & Ancient clubhouse in the background. The bridge was once a route into the ancient city of St Andrews.*

ST ANDREWS

GARY PLAYER'S VIEW

With golf-loving visitors from every corner of the globe, St Andrews is the most friendly little golf town in the world. I played my first Open Championship on the Old Course, and returned in 2000 for my 46th consecutive Open Championship appearance. You have to play the course a couple of times to understand it, as it was designed by geniuses, but I can tell you one or two things: drive carefully and, as a general rule, favour the left side of the fairways. Bring a putter you can roll the ball with a long way, as some of the greens are nearly as long as a football field. Finally, when you get to the fantastically difficult 17th 'Road Hole', pray!

ABOVE: *Gary Player with caddie Guy Gillespie at the Swilcan Bridge during the 1960 Open Championship. Player was the defending champion, having won the 1959 event at Muirfield.*

ABOVE RIGHT: *Jack Nicklaus tees off in the final round of the 1978 Open Championship at St Andrews. He shot a 3-under-par 69 to win his third Open with a total score of 281.*

standard number of holes for golf courses all over the world.

Tom Kidd won the first Open Championship to be held over the Old Course in 1873. This championship has been held here no fewer than 25 times, including the first Open of the new millennium. Golfers who have won the British Open at St Andrews – such as Bobby Jones, Sam Snead, Peter Thomson and Bobby Locke – have usually been at the peak of their careers at the time of their victory.

The greatest players of their age have always performed well here, Jack Nicklaus winning the Open in both 1970 and 1978, Seve Ballesteros in 1984, and Nick Faldo in 1990. Fittingly, it was at St Andrews that Tiger Woods became the fifth – and youngest – man to achieve the Grand Slam of Majors by winning the Open in 2000.

The Old Course is unusual in that it is set in the centre of St Andrews, with just a low white picket fence separating the course from the town itself. The early golf course layout style of nine holes out and nine holes back is preserved here, unlike modern courses which have two loops of nine holes.

The Old Course has a total of 112 bunkers, some of them notorious, like 'Hell' on the long 14th hole, 'Strath' on the short 11th, and the 'Road Hole Bunker', a particularly deep and steep-sided trap alongside the green of the par-four 17th 'Road Hole' that has ruined many a scorecard. This hole is unusual in that a road – off which the ball must be played – runs along the right side of the fairway and against the back edge of the green. Ben Crenshaw, USA Ryder Cup captain in 1999, once said: 'The Road Hole is the most difficult par four in the world because it is actually a par five.' Another interesting feature of the Old Course is its 'double greens',

first introduced in 1856. Only the 1st, 9th, 17th and 18th holes have their own greens. The rest each have two holes cut in them and can be extremely large; it is not uncommon for a golfer to be faced with a putt of almost 100m (109yd), another quirk of this unique course and one that adds to its interest and enjoyment.

ROYAL DORNOCH

Scottish links golf at its best

HIGHLAND, SCOTLAND

In the far northeast corner of Scotland, just eight degrees outside the Arctic Circle, Royal Dornoch takes one back to the misty origins of the game of golf. A course of exceptional quality and wild beauty, it has been excluded from the Open Championship roster only because of its remoteness.

Although the club itself was not founded until 1877, records show that golf has been played over this piece of barren linksland since the early 1600s; only St Andrews and Leith can claim to be older. The course remained relatively unknown until the 1960s when American golf writer Herbert Warren Wind described it in glowing terms, and it has since been visited by such top players as Gary Player, Ben Crenshaw, Tom Watson and Greg Norman.

The 6014m (6577yd) par-70 course follows the traditional layout style of nine holes out from the clubhouse and nine holes in. The first eight holes hug the inland edge of the coastline, winding through thick gorse between old dune embankments. The remaining 10 holes are played back along the coast of the Dornoch Firth, skirting the sandy beaches and exposing golfers to the full force of the stiff prevailing west wind. The course is characterized by deep pot bunkers and raised greens with fall-aways on either side that punish the errant shot.

Although Dornoch takes one back to the era of natural courses when major landscaping and reconstruction were not possible and the course was determined by the lie of the land, the layout has, at various stages in its past, been shaped by some of the most influential men in the history of the game. Royal Dornoch was originally a nine-hole course, but after 10 years Old Tom Morris was called in from St Andrews to add a further nine holes.

However, it was one of the pioneers of greenkeeping and course maintenance, and the most prominent man in Scottish golf at the time, who most shaped the devel-

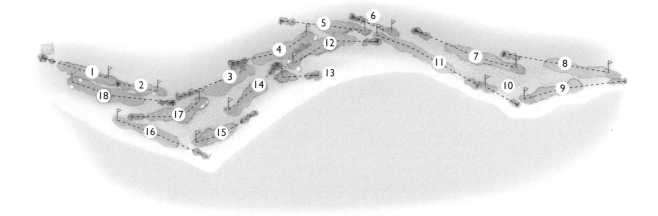

RIGHT: *The thick gorse covering the dune embankments at Royal Dornoch is attractive in full bloom, but provides a formidable hazard to golfers. Situated in a remote corner of northeast Scotland, this historic links is a course for the avid traditionalist.*

opment of the course – in 1883, Scotsman John Sutherland was appointed secretary of the club, a position he held for 50 years, and together with JH Taylor, he made several revisions to the layout. Donald Ross, the club's early greenkeeper, departed for the USA at the beginning of the new century and went on to become one of the game's greatest course architects, basing the design of many courses in the USA on Royal Dornoch – Pinehurst No. 2 being one of the best-known examples. Ross was also involved in the design of Seminole and Oakland Hills in the USA.

The first tee of the course is a stone's throw from the centre of the town of Dornoch, a cultured village just over 300km (188 miles) north of Edinburgh. Although Dornoch's remoteness ensures that its solitude will never be disrupted by the hustle and bustle of professional championship golf, the course is rated 15th in the world and the combination of classic links golf and fine scenery continues to attract a steady stream of golfing pilgrims.

Tom Watson summed it up best when he said: 'This is the most fun I've had playing golf in my whole life.' And he's played some.

ROYAL DORNOCH

GARY PLAYER'S VIEW

Royal Dornoch might be called a 'thinking man's' golf course, with wide fairways that nevertheless require intelligent placement of drives for the best shots into the pin. The signature raised plateau greens are legendary. Number two is a par three played to this type of elevated green. Tom Watson once said: 'The most difficult second shot in golf is the second to the 2nd at Royal Dornoch.' Perhaps that is another way of emphasizing the importance of chipping and pitching the ball well when playing here.

ABOVE: *The layout at Royal Dornoch hugs the coast of Dornoch Firth, exposing golfers to the force of the strong westerly wind, particularly on the back nine.*

FAR LEFT: *JH Taylor, a five-time winner of the Open Championship, together with John Sutherland, made several revisions to the Royal Dornoch layout. Taylor, along with James Braid and Harry Vardon, was a member of the famed 'Triumvirate' who among them won no less than 16 Open Championship titles. Old Tom Morris had a hand in the creation of the original course, being called in from St Andrews where he was the resident professional to design the second nine.*

BALLYBUNION (OLD)

Wild and remote

CO. KERRY, IRELAND

Deep in the county of Kerry in the southwest corner of Ireland, Ballybunion is reputed to be one of the finest links courses anywhere in the world. Because of its remoteness, it has rarely hosted professional tournaments, so there was much rejoicing when the Murphy's Irish Open was held there in 2000, Sweden's Patrik Sjöland taking the title with a 14-under par total.

The club had a difficult start. Founded in 1893, it soon found itself in severe financial difficulty and it was only five years later that retired Indian Army officer Colonel Bartholomew came to its rescue. He commissioned Lionel Hewson to lay out the first nine holes, but it was not until 1927 that the remaining nine holes were constructed and the course became a full 18-hole championship facility.

The 1st hole is a relatively simple opener with a drive to a wide fairway running downhill. Thereafter, things soon become more testing. The bunkers in the fairway of the 2nd hole make par almost impossible if found with the tee shot, while the third is a long par three played to a severely undulating green. The 7th and 8th holes are played along the clifftops which, while affording astounding views of the Atlantic Ocean, are open to mighty winds that whip off the sea. The remainder of the course meanders through sand dunes, with a small stream fronting the green of the relatively short par-five 13th. The 17th boasts possibly the course's most spectacular tee shot, played from high up with dunes on either side.

When a new clubhouse was built in 1971, the order of the holes was changed to start at what had been the 14th hole.

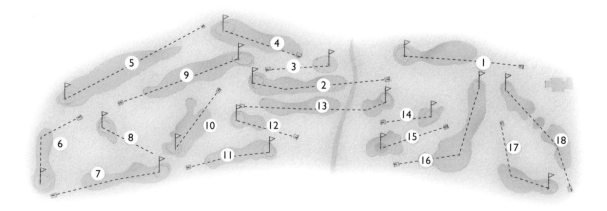

RIGHT: *The tee shot on the doglegging par-five 16th must find the fairway that runs perpendicularly and slopes upwards from the Atlantic Ocean. The green is protected by two deep bunkers on the right as players approach it.*

The bunker on that hole is still known as Mrs Simpson, named after the wife of the course architect, Tom Simpson, who tinkered with the course layout shortly before the 1937 Irish Men's Closed Championship. Simpson kept his changes to a minimum, re-siting just three greens and constructing his controversial bunker, which is placed in the middle of the fairway in the driving area.

In the late 1970s, 'Friends of Ballybunion', under the leadership of Jackie Hourigan, raised over £100,000 to save Ballybunion's cliff faces from erosion.

ABOVE: *Ballybunion's 17th, a mid-length par four played alongside the ocean, curves past a high dune to an angled green.*

BALLYBUNION

GARY PLAYER'S VIEW

Most people who have never played on a links course would probably not enjoy Ballybunion. The subtleties of this legendary design may seem hidden at first, like a pearl in an oyster shell. Yet the better you get to know the course, the more that pearl glows. Ballybunion's beauty is breathtaking, and we must accept that it is a links course designed many years ago without modern-day machinery, which accounts for its appearance of being 'untouched by man'. The challenge is to realize that golf can be played 'low to the ground,' with run-up shots to the greens and boring drives that pierce the wind — not just the high-ball target-style golf people have become used to in the USA. Ballybunion offers an experience of traditional golf at its best.

CARNOUSTIE

None so tough

ANGUS, SCOTLAND

Regarded as the toughest links course anywhere, the monster that is Carnoustie lies on the linksland near the Tay estuary on the east coast of Scotland.

The first 10 holes were laid out in about 1840 by Allan Robertson, with the final eight holes being the work of the legendary Old Tom Morris around 1857. James Braid, one of the famous 'Triumvirate', together with JH Taylor and Harry Vardon, was commissioned to revamp the course in 1926, some five years before the Open Championship was played there for the first time.

The course is brutally long at over 6700m (7300yd) and is made even tougher by the winds that whip off the sea. No more than two consecutive holes head in the same direction, so the player has to cope with the wind from all angles,

while two fast streams, Jockie's Burn and the infamous Barry Burn, also meander their way through the course.

The Open Championship has been played at Carnoustie six times since 1931, when Tommy Armour won. In 1953 Ben Hogan entered the Open for the first (and only) time, arriving at Carnoustie from the USA a full two weeks before the tournament began. From the first, he remained characteristically impassive towards the large, enthusiastic crowds he drew, earning himself the uncomplimentary nickname of 'the wee ice-mon'. In gale-force winds and intermittent rain, Hogan produced a clinical display of golf, eventually finishing with a four-round total of 282, the second-lowest total in Open Championship history at that time. It was not until 1968 that the Open was again played at Carnoustie,

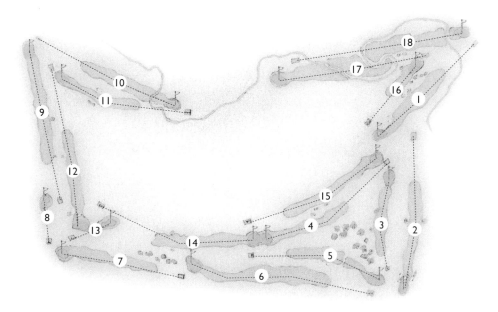

RIGHT: *The par-five 6th hole at Carnoustie was birdied twice by American Ben Hogan in his victorious (and only) visit to the Open Championship in 1953. The unusual route he took is now known as Hogan's Alley.*

when Gary Player was the one to triumph. Then, in 1975, Tom Watson won the first of his five Open Championships.

For 24 years Carnoustie was ignored as a venue for the Open, mainly because of its lack of accommodation facilities and therefore its inability to cope with the huge influx of players, officials and spectators. With the building of the stunning new hotel overlooking the 18th green, many of these problems have been solved and 1999 saw Carnoustie return as an Open venue.

The 1999 Open will be forever remembered for two things. Firstly, the rough was allowed to grow punitively thick and the fairways were as narrow as 13.7m (15yd) in places. Scores ballooned and vociferous criticism of the farcical nature of the course setup was rampant. Spanish teenage sensation Sergio Garcia's reputation took a knock when he opened with an 89 in the first round, following with an 83 for a two-round total of 172, missing the cut by 20 shots.

Secondly, it will be remembered for the spectacular collapse of Frenchman Jean van de Velde who blew a three-shot lead on the final hole, his ball finding a watery grave in

the Barry Burn on the 18th hole – proving that water need only be a few metres wide to be a devastatingly effective design feature. Little-known Scotsman Paul Lawrie went on to win the four-hole playoff against van de Velde and American Justin Leonard to record his first Major victory.

LEFT: *The 155m (168yd) par-three 13th is protected by a large bean-shaped bunker in front of the green.*

TOP: *A view back down the 18th fairway showing the notorious Barry Burn which crosses the fairway short of the green.*

ABOVE RIGHT: *Scotland's Paul Lawrie won the 1999 Open Championship at Carnoustie, having triumphed in a three-way playoff involving himself, Frenchman Jean van de Velde and Justin Leonard of the USA.*

CARNOUSTIE
GARY PLAYER'S VIEW

Carnoustie is probably the toughest course I have ever played, even though I managed to win the Open Championship here in 1968. It is long and well bunkered, with undulating fairways. When the wind whips off the Tay estuary, it feels like 6700m (7300yd) of headache! It has a 'working person's' soul; nothing pretty or dainty about it. It also has one of Scotland's most famous hazards, the Barry Burn.

MUIRFIELD

Home of 'gentlemen of honour'

GULLANE, EAST LOTHIAN, SCOTLAND

Although Muirfield has hosted the Open Championship no fewer than 14 times since the course was opened in 1891, the 88th Open in 1959 will always remain special to Gary Player. The 23-year-old Player opened badly, carding a 75 on day one, but improving slightly on day two with a 71 to make the cut by two strokes. Day three saw the young South African card a fighting 70 for a total of 217, four strokes behind the leaders, Britons Fred Bullock and Sam King, joining a group of 13 players on 217 or better.

After a promising start on the front nine on day four, where he shot a 34, Player seemed set to return an even better score on the back nine – a par on the par-four 18th would give him a 32 for a round of 66 and a realistic shot at

the title. But Player hit his drive into one of Muirfield's many bunkers and then three-putted to drop two shots for a 68 and a total of 284.

Player left the 18th green in tears, believing he had let the Championship slip from his grasp. However, one by one, the leaders out on the course dropped away, with Bullock and Belgian Flory van Donck eventually finishing on 286. Player had just become the youngest Open Champion since Willie Auchterlonie in 1893.

Muirfield is home to one of the world's oldest golf clubs, the Honourable Company of Edinburgh Golfers, formed in 1744 when 'several Gentlemen of Honour skilful in the ancient and healthful exercise of Golf' approached the

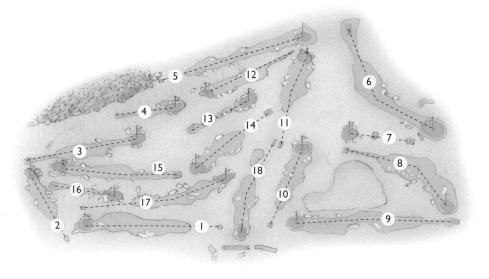

LEFT: *This view of the green of the par-four 3rd hole at Muirfield shows the characteristic openness of the layout and the harsh rough awaiting the miss-hit shot. In 1892 Muirfield hosted the first 72-hole Open Championship.*

RIGHT: *The green of Muirfield's par-three 13th hole is guarded by three fearsome bunkers. With more than 160 bunkers, many of them with steep turf walls, Muirfield is a private course and is home to the exclusive Honourable Company of Edinburgh Golfers.*

Edinburgh City Council to donate a silver club as a prize for their annual competition on the Leith links. In later years, the exclusive club moved twice in search of less crowded golfing facilities, eventually settling in Gullane, along the coast east of Edinburgh where the present Muirfield course was laid out by Old Tom Morris and opened for play in 1891. Muirfield hosted the Open Championship the following year, the first time the event was played over 72 holes.

Since those early days, and due in some part to changes made by Harry Colt and Tom Simpson in the 1920s, Muirfield has evolved into one of the world's most respected championship courses. It has earned a reputation as one of the fairest on the Open Championship roster, with few trees and no blind shots, hidden bunkers or water hazards. However, its extensive, deep bunkering (there are over 160 bunkers, many with walls of sod turf) and severe rough ensure a challenge worthy of the world's best golfers.

And the world's best have risen to the challenge over the years. The great Harry Vardon won at Muirfield in 1896, while James Braid won the Claret Jug here in both 1901

and 1906. Walter Hagen won his fourth and final Open on this course in 1929, while Henry Cotton won here in 1948 with a superb display of driving. In addition, American Jack Nicklaus recorded the first of his three Open victories at Muirfield in 1966 and went on to name his own course in Dublin, Ohio (USA), Muirfield Village after the Scottish course.

One of the most dramatic finishes in British Open golf came at Muirfield in 1972 when Mexican Lee Trevino chipped in from the rough for par on the par-five 17th. Briton Tony Jacklin, at that stage level with Trevino and well-positioned on the green for a birdie or par, was so shaken that he three-putted to hand Trevino the title.

While Muirfield's convenient location has seen it host many championship events, including the 1973 Ryder Cup, it is not a public course like the great links courses of St Andrews and Carnoustie. The exclusive Honourable Company of Edinburgh Golfers guards the course's privacy as jealously as it does the traditions of the game, ensuring the club's members play their golf on quiet and uncrowded fairways.

MUIRFIELD
GARY PLAYER'S VIEW

Muirfield has a special place in my heart as I won my first Open there. It is a demanding driving golf course, yet overall a fair test of championship-calibre golf. The course is beautifully bunkered and, as a links course, plays tougher when the breeze blows off the sea. However, it is so skilfully designed that even on calm days its deep traps more than adequately defend the course.

ABOVE: *A young Gary Player lifts the Claret Jug for the first time after winning the Open championship at Muirfield in 1959.*

LEFT: *The clubhouse at Muirfield overlooks the green of one of the toughest finishing holes in golf, the long par-four 18th.*

ROYAL TROON

Licking the 'Postage Stamp'

AYRSHIRE, SCOTLAND

Royal Troon, on the west coast of Scotland, is recognized as one of the toughest courses on the British Open roster. The prevailing wind is from the northwest and, as is typical in many links courses, the holes follow a nine-out and nine-back layout. This means that golfers set out with the wind at their backs, but are faced with the full force of the Ayrshire weather on the homeward journey, making this long course (6489m; 7097yd) an exceptionally stern test.

For many years, Troon boasted both the longest and shortest holes in Open Championship golf. What was once the longest, the 6th is a fearsome par five at 527m (577yd). Even in favourable conditions, it is difficult to reach the green in two, and when the wind is blowing it is downright impossible. The shortest hole is the 115m (126yd) par-three 8th. Sometimes it may require no more than a wedge to find the green but, if the wind comes up off the Firth of Clyde, it may demand as much as a three-iron. The hole is called the 'Postage Stamp' because of the size of its green,

but the saying goes that unlike a normal postage stamp, this one is not easily licked.

It is best remembered for two contrasting incidents. During the 1950 Open, German amateur Hermann Tissies took 15 on this hole, although he only had one putt. His tee shot found one of the 'Postage Stamp' green's five deep bunkers. He needed five strokes to escape, only to find a similarly difficult bunker on the opposite side of the small green. Another five strokes saw him return to the original bunker, from where he required another three to escape, before one-putting for 15.

American Gene Sarazen played in his first British Open in 1923, which was also the year Troon first hosted the event. Although Sarazen was the reigning US Open and US PGA champion, he failed to make the cut at Troon after a bout of typical Ayrshire coast weather saw his day-two score balloon to 85.

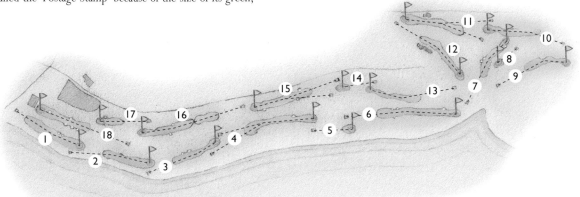

RIGHT: *Royal Troon's par-five 6th is named Turnberry. At 527m (577yd) it is one of the longest holes encountered on the Open rota. The landing area off the tee is guarded by a triangle of cavernous bunkers, while the green is long, narrow and raised.*

Half a century later, on the 50th anniversary of the first Open at Troon, Sarazen – who had gone on to become the first player to take the Grand Slam of all four modern Majors – was invited to participate in the 1973 Open Championship. Then 71, he played his tee shot at the 'Postage Stamp' on day one with a five-iron: the ball pitched just short of the hole and rolled in for a hole-in-one. The following day, Sarazen again played a five-iron, but found a greenside bunker. The man who had invented the sand wedge climbed down to play his recovery shot – and it went straight into the hole for a remarkable birdie! Although he went on to miss the cut in the event, the memory of those shots will live forever. Sarazen presented his five-iron to the Royal & Ancient Golf Club of St Andrews, where it is still on display today.

Royal Troon has hosted the Open on seven occasions. Arthur Havers won the first event in 1923, and a host of illustrious golfers have since gone on to win here. In 1950, South African Bobby Locke won with a score of 279, the first time 280 had been broken in the tournament's history, and defending champion Arnold Palmer set a record score of 276 in 1962. Tom Weiskopf equalled Palmer's score to win in 1973, while Tom Watson collected the fourth of his five Open titles at Royal Troon in 1982. American Mark Calcavecchia held off Australian Greg Norman and Wayne Grady in the Open's first four-hole playoff in 1989, while American Justin Leonard was a gracious and popular victor in 1997.

Golf was first played over this piece of land as early as 1870, but it was not until 1878 that the club was established. The present layout has been influenced by several notable course architects: the 1883 Open champion, Willie Fernie, made various alterations to the layout during his tenure as club professional, while James Braid, Dr Alister Mackenzie and Frank Penninck also made significant contributions.

ROYAL TROON

GARY PLAYER'S VIEW

Royal Troon greets you with a very 'normal' and benign front nine, but the back nine is as difficult a group of holes as I have ever experienced. Royal Troon provides an unusual experience since it requires you to hit long-carrying tee shots over high sand dunes that block your line of sight. In other words, you often do not have a clear idea as to where you are playing or just where your tee shot lands.

TOP: *Gene Sarazen (left) and Bobby Jones pictured in 1923, the year in which Royal Troon hosted its first Open. Americans have won the last five Opens played at Troon: Palmer, Weiskopf, Watson, Calcavecchia and Leonard.*

LEFT: *Royal Troon's par-three 8th, the so-called 'Postage Stamp', is at 115m (126yd) the shortest hole in Open Championship golf. The tiny green is surrounded by five yawning bunkers, and a very uncertain lie awaits in long grass low to the right of the green.*

TURNBERRY

In the shadow of Ailsa Craig

AILSA COURSE, AYRSHIRE, SCOTLAND

At the southernmost end of a stretch of classic linksland on Scotland's Ayrshire coast lies Turnberry, the site of one of the world's most beautiful and challenging golf courses. High on a hill overlooking Turnberry's Ailsa course is the famous Turnberry Hotel. Looming from the Firth of Clyde behind the links is the stark silhouette of Ailsa Craig, a huge round island of granite, while the Isle of Arran and the Mull of Kintyre can be seen beyond.

Turnberry has a long and eventful past and has, in recent years, been the scene of dramatic golfing moments in its short championship history. The third Marquis of Ailsa leased the land at Turnberry to the Glasgow and South Western Railway Company, and 1883 Open champion Willie Fernie, then the professional at nearby Troon, finished designing two 13-hole courses on the site in 1905. The Turnberry Hotel was built at the same time.

Turnberry's rise to championship status was delayed when, during World War I, the Royal Flying Corps built a training airfield on the site. Although the course was restored after the war – when a second layout, the Arran course, was also built – it was again severely damaged during World War II when the Royal Air Force built an airfield over the courses. Thanks to the efforts of Frank Hole and McKenzie Ross, the course was rebuilt and restored to its former glory in the years following the war. Remnants of the airfields can still be seen on the course, and a monument to the 119 airmen who died while stationed at Turnberry during the two wars stands beside the 12th green.

Soon after its restoration, Turnberry was awarded championship status, hosting the Scottish Championships and the News of the World Matchplay in the 1950s, as well as the Amateur Championship in 1961. It was some years, however, before it was included on the Open roster. It

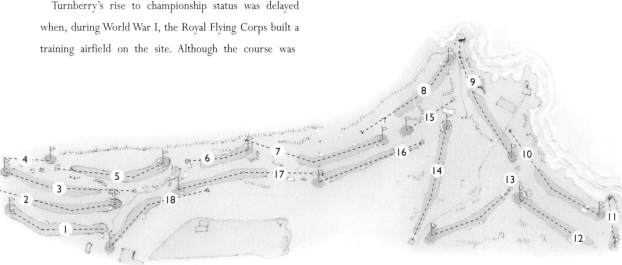

RIGHT: *Turnberry's par-four 8th hole doglegs left along Turnberry Bay to a raised, two-tiered green guarded by three bunkers. Tom Watson was Turnberry's first Open champion when he won the event in 1977, beating Jack Nicklaus in the famous 'Duel in the Sun'.*

hosted its first Open in 1977, which saw one of the most dramatic head-to-head battles in championship golf.

Known as the 'Duel in the Sun', it was a battle between Americans Jack Nicklaus, aged 37, and Tom Watson, aged 27, fighting for the Claret Jug and the position of number one golfer in the world. Nicklaus, the master, and Watson, the pretender to the throne, matched each other shot for shot, both shooting rounds of 68 on day one, 70 on day two, and 65 on day three, leaving the rest of the field far behind.

Although Nicklaus began day four with two birdies to pull ahead, Watson fought back and, after 16 holes in the final round, the pair were still level. Then Watson birdied the par-five 17th to take the lead for the first time. A spellbound gallery watched as Watson's drive found the fairway on the par-four 18th while Nicklaus's drive ran into the rough on the right. Watson hit a seven-iron to within five feet to set up a birdie, while Nicklaus played a fine recovery shot from the long grass to lie 11m (12yd) from the pin. Playing, as Peter Ryde wrote in *The Times*, 'with the courage of despair', Nicklaus miraculously holed his birdie putt, but an implacable Watson, needing the birdie, calmly rolled in his five-footer for a championship record of 268 and his second Open title.

Watson went on to become the world's top golfer soon after this victory at Turnberry, as did Australian Greg Norman after he won his first Major – the 1986 Open Championship at Turnberry. Eight years later, Zimbabwean Nick Price, the dominant golfer of the early 1990s, laid to rest the ghosts of missed opportunity at Royal Troon in 1982 when he finished eagle-birdie-par at Turnberry to edge out Swede Jesper Parnevik and claim the Claret Jug. Turnberry's Open winners have been golfers reaching the pinnacle of their abilities and, as such, they are fitting champions for one of Scotland's most outstanding golf courses.

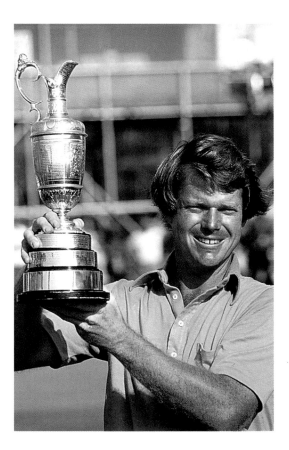

TURNBERRY
GARY PLAYER'S VIEW

This is a favourite of mine, and I am proud to have won the Senior British Open Championship here. Two famous landmarks grace the course, a lighthouse close to the 9th tee and a distant mass of rock, the Ailsa Craig, that rises from the Firth of Clyde. This is a magical spot that people have compared to Pebble Beach and Cypress Point. The hotel sits high on the hill from where you look right over the ocean to see the entire golf course.

ABOVE: *Tom Watson won his second Open Championship title at Turnberry in 1977. Today Watson's name appears on the Claret Jug five times, having won the event for the last time in 1983.*

ABOVE LEFT: *The lighthouse at Turnberry stands on a rocky headland jutting into the Firth of Clyde. It was built in 1873 by Robert Louis Stevenson's father, a renowned engineer.*

ROYAL BIRKDALE

England's premier championship layout

SOUTHPORT, LANCASHIRE, ENGLAND

Royal Birkdale, on England's Lancashire coast, has hosted over 30 championships and international matches since World War II, making it the most important tournament venue in England. Most recently, it played host to the 1998 Open Championship, an event won by American Mark O'Meara, who had also won the Masters earlier that year, and had set the course record of 64 at Royal Birkdale in 1987.

Birkdale has a history of worthy Open champions. Peter Thomson won his (and Birkdale's) first Open in 1954 and it was also here, in 1965, that the Australian held up the Claret Jug for the fifth and final time. In 1961, American Arnold Palmer powered his way to victory at Royal Birkdale after playing what is undoubtedly his most famous shot. On what was then the 15th hole – it is now the 16th – Palmer drove the ball into the rough, where it came to rest under a bush 135m (150yd) from the green. He seemed set to drop a shot but, in an astonishing display of brute strength, he played a six-iron out of the bush, over the bunkers and onto the green. The shot is commemorated by a plaque in the rough at the 16th, marked by a rose bush.

In 1971, Mexican Lee Trevino was a popular winner of the 100th Championship when he beat Taiwan's Lu Liang

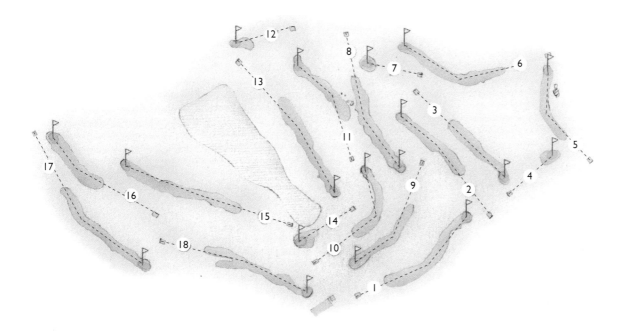

RIGHT: *A new 12th hole, nestling among rolling sand hills, was constructed at Royal Birkdale in 1965, the year in which the course hosted both the Ryder Cup and the Open Championship – which was won by Australian Peter Thomson.*

Huan (or 'Mr Lu' as he was affectionately known by the crowds at Birkdale). It was Trevino's third victory in 23 days, following his success in both the US and Canadian Opens.

Although American Johnny Miller managed, in 1976, to overtake three-day leader Seve Ballesteros to claim victory, it was the young Spaniard who dominated the headlines during that week at Birkdale, which effectively launched his career. The 1983 Open saw another five-time winner, American Tom Watson, lift the Claret Jug, while in 1991 a relatively unknown Australian, Ian Baker-Finch, held off the challenges of Mark O'Meara and Ballesteros to clinch victory – a golden moment in a career that has never again reached such heights.

First opened in 1889, Royal Birkdale was a nine-hole layout just over a kilometre from the current 18 holes. Eight years later, George Lowe from neighbouring Royal Lytham & St Annes was brought in to oversee construction of the new Birkdale course. The layout has seen several revisions over its long history. In 1932, FG Hawtree and former Open Champion JH Taylor remodelled the course to turn Birkdale into a tough championship course. They threaded the fairways through the valleys between the giant, scrub-covered sand hills rather than over the top of them, thus avoiding the undulating fairways and blind tee shots typical of links courses. It was also at this time that the new clubhouse was constructed, with wide windows looking out over the course towards the Irish Sea.

Maintaining the family connection, FG Hawtree's son, Fred, was brought in to remodel the course again in 1963 and, in 1991, following complaints about the greens during

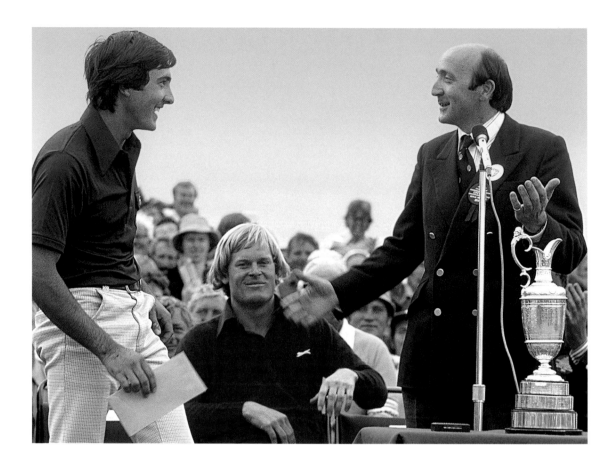

that year's Open, a third generation of Hawtrees was called upon. Golf course architect Martin Hawtree, son of Fred and grandson of FG Hawtree, was given the task of reconstructing Birkdale's greens. He created what is rated as one of the fairest championship courses, with only one blind tee shot – at the 9th hole. Unusually, the course is made up of three loops, with the 9th, 14th and 18th greens situated near the clubhouse. Before the 1998 Championship, further changes were made. Most notably, 6000 white pines were

removed from the course with a view to restoring the links feel of the layout. In addition, several holes were made longer, pushing the length of the course off the championship tees to a challenging 6417m (7018yd). With this new, open layout ideal for the viewing public, and its length and exposure to the sea winds ensuring that it is kept tougher than ever for the players, Birkdale seems set to maintain its position on the championship roster well into the 21st century.

ABOVE RIGHT: *A young Seve Ballesteros of Spain (left) accepts the runner-up cheque while winner Johnny Miller of the USA waits to receive the Claret Jug after winning his first and only Open Championship at Royal Birkdale in 1976. Ballesteros went on to win the event in 1979 at Royal Lytham & St Annes, in 1984 at St Andrews and for the last time in 1988, again at Royal Lytham & St Annes.*

RIGHT: *Royal Birkdale's fairways are laid out in the valleys between scrub and gorse-covered sand hills.*

ROYAL BIRKDALE
GARY PLAYER'S VIEW

Golf writers often link my victory in the 1959 Open Championship at Muirfield and Arnold Palmer's at Royal Birkdale in 1961 as the catalyst that made people see the Open as a truly international event. Birkdale has undulating terrain and dunes with plentiful scrub. The rough is thick, and you sometimes have to play out of the Scottish-style bunkers backwards because of their severely steeped faces. Wind and rain, along with the absence of potentially unfair blind shots, make it one of the world's truest tests of golf.

ROYAL LYTHAM & ST ANNES
An inland links

Royal Lytham & St Annes Golf Club is situated in Lytham St Annes, just outside Blackpool on England's west coast, bordering the Irish Sea.

Originally built (with an adjoining nine holes for ladies) on a piece of linksland leased from the St-Annes-on-Sea Land and Building Company in 1886, the club moved to its present site on the Fylde Coast in 1897. George Lowe is credited with the original course design, although course architects such as Harry Colt, Herbert Fowler and CK Cotton have had a hand in changes carried out over the years.

The substantial Victorian clubhouse was opened in 1898 after some 750 members raised what was then an enormous amount of £8500. It still stands today, overlooking the 18th green which is so close that in 1974 Gary Player was forced to play a third shot left-handed, using the back of his putter from against the wall after his approach ran through the green.

The course has been on the Open Championship roster since 1926 when Bobby Jones won the first of his three Open victories there.

Although now some distance from the sea, Royal Lytham has all the characteristics of a typical links course, with its links grasses, pot bunkers and undulating fairways and several blind tee shots. The course does not, however, run in the traditional links layout of the first nine heading outwards and the second nine returning in the opposite direction. The routing changes direction no fewer than 12 times. Additional oddities are that the round opens with a par three and there are back-to-back par fives at the 6th and 7th holes, while the back nine has only one par three and one par five.

At first sight, the layout seems fairly benign, but crosswinds can make judgement of distances extremely tricky. Royal Lytham & St Annes is famed for its seemingly out-of-place bunkers, many of which appear to be in laughable positions. Depending on the wind, however, they are all strategically positioned so as to be able to catch the casual or wayward shot.

LEFT: *A view down the fairway of the par-four 18th at Royal Lytham & St Annes. The putting surface is situated within metres of the imposing Victorian clubhouse. To the left is the tee of the 1st, unusually a par three, and beyond, the Dormy House which offers accommodation.*

The par-four 15th is a perfect example of just how tough the course can be. It measures a little over 430m (470yd) into the wind, and, for three days of the 1974 Open, the stroke average of the field was more than a shot over par.

Royal Lytham & St Annes has now hosted the Open Championship on nine occasions, on two of which the victor was a South African (Bobby Locke in 1952 and Gary Player in 1974). Australian star Peter Thomson won in 1958 and the New Zealand left-hander, Bob Charles, triumphed in 1963. In 1969, Tony Jacklin became the first Briton to win the Open in 18 years, and Seve Ballesteros won both in 1979 and 1988. In 1996, Tom Lehman became the first American professional to win the Open at Royal Lytham & St Annes when he triumphed over Mark McCumber and South Africa's Ernie Els.

ABOVE: *A plaque commemorates the astonishing shot on the 17th that enabled Bobby Jones to win the 1926 Open.*

TOP LEFT: *Seve Ballesteros plays his tee shot at the short 9th during the 1988 Open Championship, which he went on to win in rather more conventional manner than he did in 1979, when his wild driving was rescued by miraculous recovery shots.*

TOP RIGHT: *Pot bunkers in the traditional manner litter the course, and every single green is strongly protected by them.*

ROYAL LYTHAM & ST ANNES
GARY PLAYER'S VIEW

When Hale Irwin played here for the first time he said it was like playing on the moon. The undulating, sloping fairways dance all over the place, so each shot is a test in itself. The front nine is reasonably short, but the back nine is very long and always plays into the wind. I won the Open Championship here in 1974, not without a little drama. On the last day, my iron approach shot hit the green on the 18th and bounced over. The ball came to rest against a wall that fronts the clubhouse. I had to turn my putter around and hit the ball back to the green left-handed.

ROYAL ST GEORGE'S
Southern England's only Open venue

SANDWICH, KENT, ENGLAND

Royal St George's is one of England's greatest and most historic links golf courses, hosting the first ever Open Championship to be played in England as well as on 11 subsequent occasions. The first tournament in 1894 also saw the first victory by an Englishman, JH Taylor, marking the start of the domination of this event by Taylor, James Braid and Harry Vardon, who became known as the Great Triumvirate.

Royal St George's was clearly a course to Taylor's liking, as he went on to become the first man to break 70 in an Open here in 1904. Between them, the Great Triumvirate won 16 of a total of 21 Open Championships played between 1894 and 1914.

Vardon recorded two of these victories at Royal St George's, while the great Walter Hagen won two of his four Open titles here, in 1922 and 1928. The course was also the scene of South African Bobby Locke's victory in 1949.

More recently, in 1985, Sandy Lyle became the first British winner of the event in 16 years at Royal St George's. World number one at the time, Greg Norman of Australia won his second Open here in 1993, despite Payne Stewart's fourth-round 63 which tied for the lowest round ever in a British Open.

Situated among towering sand hills overlooking Pegwell Bay in southern England, Royal St George's was built by Dr Laidlaw Purves, a Scot who had moved down from Edinburgh in the 1880s. Inland golf courses were not highly regarded at that time, and Purves was looking for a suitable seaside site to construct a Scottish-style links course for London golfers. Regarding the piece of land near the village of Sandwich as perfect, he formed the Sandwich Golfing Association in 1887 and proceeded to lay out a golf course. Despite the occasional modification over the years, the course today remains essentially true to the original layout.

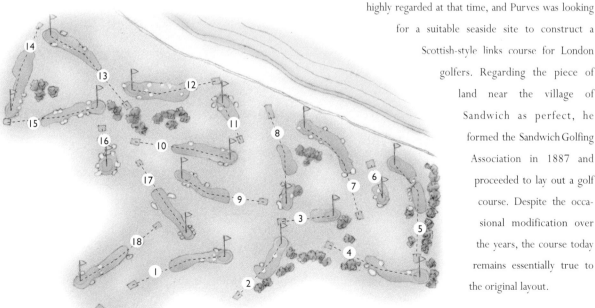

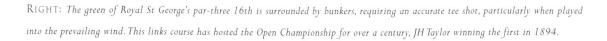

RIGHT: *The green of Royal St George's par-three 16th is surrounded by bunkers, requiring an accurate tee shot, particularly when played into the prevailing wind. This links course has hosted the Open Championship for over a century, JH Taylor winning the first in 1894.*

ROYAL ST GEORGE'S
GARY PLAYER'S VIEW

Close to the sea and overlooking Pegwell Bay, Royal St George's is transformed from tough into an even tougher challenge with any kind of wind. The sweeping rough at the 1st hole can be daunting, as can the bunkers and huge sand hills that can kick the ball off in unpredictable bounces and frustrate even the most patient player. There is so much danger here when the wind picks up off the channel — especially on holes 4 through 8 — that your potentially best score for a round can turn into a nightmare on a single hole. Yet a good round completed here feels that much more satisfying and rewarding.

Playing to a par of 70, Royal St George's measures 6337m (6930yd) off the back tees and is characterized by undulating fairways that often result in the ball coming to rest on a slope. Sea breezes off the bay add to the challenge.

Royal St George's is perhaps best remembered for what has become known as the 'bottle shot'. During the 1949 Open Championship, Ireland's Harry Bradshaw was at the top of the leader-board during the final round when he played his approach shot to the par-four 5th. His ball came to rest inside a broken beer bottle behind the green. According to the Rules of Golf, Bradshaw would have been allowed to take a free drop, which probably would have seen him putting for par. However, unaware of this particular rule, he chose to play the ball as it lay, smashing it out of the bottle and eventually carding a double-bogey six. At the end of regulation play, he found himself tied on 283 with Bobby Locke, who then went on to beat him in the playoff.

ABOVE: *Ireland's Harry Bradshaw came close to an Open Championship victory at Royal St George's in 1949. He tied with South Africa's Bobby Locke after 72 holes of regulation play, having carded a double-bogey six on the 5th after playing the infamous 'bottle shot'.*

RIGHT: *A thatched starter's hut and a bell post flank the 1st tee at Royal St George's. A short drive at this hole will leave the golfer with a difficult long second shot to be played out of the hollow known as 'The Kitchen'.*

PORTMARNOCK

An honest test of skill

CO. DUBLIN, IRELAND

Situated across an estuary from Sutton in County Dublin, Ireland, the course at Portmarnock was set up by WC Pickeman and George Ross, who rowed across the estuary to the remote spot to construct it on the site of an earlier course – of sorts – owned by the Jameson family of Irish whiskey fame. Pickeman and a man named Mungo Park designed the first nine holes of the new course in 1894, with the other nine completed four years later. Yet another nine holes were laid out by Fred W Hawtree in 1970.

Naturally, the course is accessible by road today, but when Pickeman and Ross made the journey it was by ferry, about which there are many legends. One recounts the story of the intolerant club ferryman's disagreement with a passenger who was a clergyman of a different religious faith. Apparently, the ferryman refused to let him out at his destination, which was the Portmarnock course.

The course itself is typical of a links course, exposed to the elements, with weather that can change within the space of a few hours from sunny and benign to a howling storm. The original course was just some 5304m (5800yd) but, with advances in golf equipment, both clubs and balls, the championship course has since been extended to just over 6400m (7000yd). Of the 12 par fours, five are longer than 374m (410yd), while two of the three par fives measure well over 500m (550yd).

The course has played host to many important tournaments over the years, including the British Amateur Championship in 1949. Portmarnock has also been the

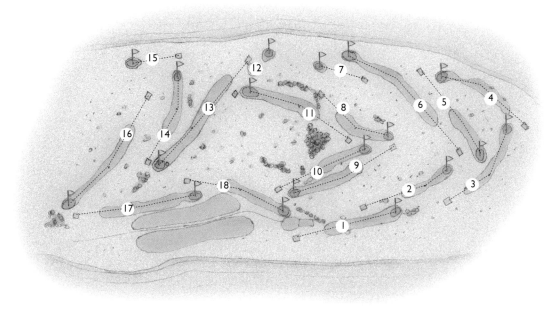

RIGHT: *The par-five 6th hole, measuring 550m (605yd), is one of three par fives at Portmarnock that measure more than 475m (520yd). Scotland's Sandy Lyle set the course record of 64 at Portmarnock during the 1989 Irish Open.*

venue for the Irish Open on numerous occasions, such as in 1988 and 1989, when Welshman Ian Woosnam won with identical scores of 278. In 1987, Germany's Bernhard Langer took full advantage of the benign conditions to post four rounds in the 60s, his worst round being 68 for a four-round total of 269 – 19 shots under par.

The course's signature hole is probably the par-four 14th that runs towards the Irish Sea. It has a deep bunker on the left of the fairway to catch wayward drives as well as a series of bunkers that guard the small raised green. This is followed by the spectacular 174m (190yd) par-three 15th that runs parallel to the beach. It is said that successfully negotiating these two holes is critical to achieve a respectable score at Portmarnock.

Because it has no hidden challenges, Portmarnock is considered to be an honest test of skill without reliance on modern design trickeries.

PORTMARNOCK
GARY PLAYER'S VIEW

Located just outside Dublin, Portmarnock is not only one of the world's best golf courses, but also one of my favourites despite being demanding. Like the courses in the Open Championship rotation, it is a typical links course, so there is usually plenty of wind, extremely well thought-out pot bunkers, deceptively tricky greens and high rough. When the wind is down, however, it can play serenely: without having to battle the elements, a player has the opportunity to think his way around the layout more patiently.

RIGHT: *The par-three 15th at Portmarnock is one of several holes that border the Irish Sea and is consequently exposed and vulnerable to the constantly changing weather conditions – a tough handful even for the professionals.*

ROYAL COUNTY DOWN

A majestic links

Situated in the coastal town of Newcastle, some 50km (30 miles) south of Belfast in Northern Ireland, the Royal County Down links course is considered by many to be one of the world's toughest. The course lies around the curve of Dundrum Bay and on a clear day the view stretches to the peak of Slieve Donard, the Isle of Man more than 60km (37 miles) to the east and, on the other side, the hills of Ballynahinch.

According to the minutes of the club, founded in March 1889, it was Old Tom Morris of St Andrews who, for the princely sum of four golden guineas, converted an existing nine holes largely created by nature and left recommendations for an additional nine.

The course has seen numerous changes during its many years of existence. In 1904, its professional, Seymour Dunn, suggested amendments, as did Harry Vardon in 1908. The last significant alterations were made by Harry Colt in 1926, but all who have worked on the course have preserved the very natural feel of this wonderful site, not least by retaining a number of blind shots.

Unlike many of the links courses which go out and back, Royal County Down has two nine-hole loops of entirely different character. This is thanks to George Combe, a founder member of the club who spent many years as chairman of the greens committee. The layout is a traditionalist's paradise: down either side of the narrow fairways are high sandhills giving each hole a sense of privacy and uniqueness.

The first three holes run northward along the beach that fringes Dundrum Bay, where the sand hills are thickly clad

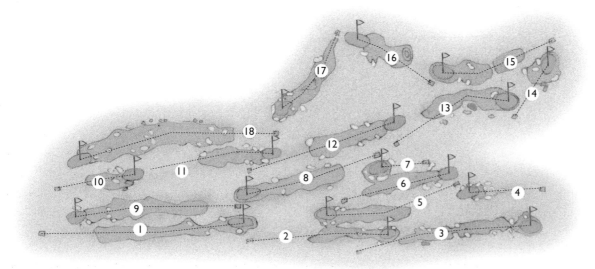

RIGHT: *Although more than 180m (200yd) long, the par-three 4th is not the toughest of County Down's par threes — even though 10 penal bunkers await wayward shots. In the distance are Dundrum Bay and the Mountains of Mourne.*

in grasping gorse and heather – meaning that off-target shots are easily lost. The battering winds off the Irish Sea present a complicating challenge since the sheer size of the dunes means that the ball is protected for parts of its flight, and exposed for others.

Another challenge is that as many as five tee shots are played blind towards aiming markers, and on a number of holes the approach to the green is at least partially obscured. An idiosyncratic feature of the bunkers is that they are fringed by reedy grass eyebrows, adding to their wild and fierce aspect and making escape from them harder.

Three of the par threes are more than 183m (200yd) long, with bunkers, gorse and heavy rough that severely punishes any wayward shots. Among the par fives, only the 9th is less than 457m (500yd), with the finishing hole closer to 503m (550yd). Despite the length of these holes, the overall course length is only 6372m (6968yd) for the par-72 layout.

Because of its relative remoteness Royal County Down has staged few major events, but in 1970 Michael Bonallack crowned a distinguished playing career by taking his fifth Amateur Championship there. The championship returned in 1999, when Graeme Storm emerged victorious.

ROYAL COUNTY DOWN
GARY PLAYER'S VIEW

This may be the finest golf course in Ireland. It is not only one of the world's best, but also one of the most beautiful. There is a hallowed atmosphere here not unlike that at St Andrews, and they say Mother Nature was the architect, with some assistance from Old Tom Morris. The course has quite a few blind rises and is long and tough, particularly when your ball finds the yellow gorse or purple heather colourfully, but treacherously, lining the fairways. In addition, the rounded greens are very fast.

Royal County Down hosted the 2000 Senior British Open, Christy O'Connor Jnr successfully defending the title.

ABOVE: *Royal County Down is one of the few links courses that boasts spectacular scenery, as is evident here around the curve of Dundrum Bay. Although largely shaped by nature, the original course was laid out by Old Tom Morris in 1889.*

ROYAL PORTRUSH

Home of 'Calamity Corner'

CO. ANTRIM, NORTHERN IRELAND

Royal Portrush, situated in Portrush, County Antrim, is one of three royal courses in Northern Ireland. The club was founded in May 1888 by Colonel JM McCalmont and JS Alexander, known as the Admiral of Portlenone. Five years later, the club was granted royal patronage by the Duke of York and became the Royal Portrush Golf Club, with the Prince of Wales (later King Edward VII) as patron.

The earliest and most famous course lies near the ruins of its namesake, Dunluce Castle. The first nine holes were laid out in 1888 with another nine being added the following year. Back then, eight holes were laid out on the land side of the coastal road that leads to the famous rock formations of the Giant's Causeway but, over the years, substantial changes have seen the course move further out into the dunes towards the sea. From the highest point of these dunes the player catches glimpses of the hills of Donegal in the west, the Isle of Islay and the Southern Hebrides in the north, and the Giant's Causeway and the Skerries to the east.

Dunluce's fairways are extremely narrow, with all holes except the 1st and 18th doglegging fairly severely one way or the other. Although the spectacular green of the par-four 5th 'hangs' on the edge of a cliff, it is the par-three 14th that is probably Ireland's

most famous. Depending on the wind, its 192m (210yd) can require anything from a medium-iron to a well-struck driver to reach the putting surface, which features a chasm to its right – giving the hole its well-deserved name of 'Calamity Corner'.

In 1951, Royal Portrush hosted the Open Championship – the only Irish course to have been afforded this singular honour – with Max Faulkner taking the title. The course record of 66 around the 6108m (6680yd) par-73 layout was set in the same year by Jack Hargreaves.

The Valley Course, a layout especially suited to ladies' golf, lies between the East Strand and the Dunluce Course and is home to the Royal Portrush Ladies Club and the affiliated Rathmore Club.

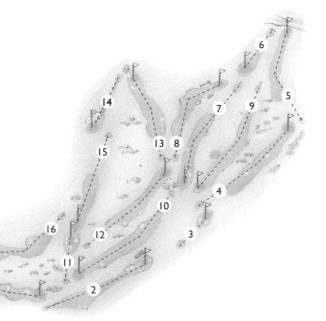

RIGHT: *From the fairway of Royal Portrush's par-five 2nd, the town of Portrush in County Antrim can be seen in the background. The course has hosted the Open Championship on one occasion, when England's Max Faulkner won his only Open title.*

ROYAL PORTRUSH
GARY PLAYER'S VIEW

This course has perhaps not received the recogni-tion it deserves, partly because of its location on the remote Antrim coast north of Belfast. One of the great golf courses of the world, it presents a fine balance of holes and superb putting greens. Cut with great naturalness amongst the sand dunes, it plays along high cliffs offering spectacular views of the water below. The 14th hole, 'Calamity Corner', calls for a long shot across a grassy chasm — an extreme challenge, especially in the wind.

ABOVE: *The corner of the sharp dogleg 13th is guarded by three bunkers. Another guards the green short left.*

LEFT: *The par-three 14th, one of the most famous holes in Ireland, is known as Calamity Corner. Here the tee shot demands anything from a medium-iron to a driver, depending on the wind.*

SHINNECOCK HILLS

A 'Scottish links' in America

SOUTHAMPTON, NEW YORK STATE, USA

The game of golf began its expansion from the remote coastal courses of Scotland to the far reaches of the earth in the early 19th century – first to England, then, following British explorers and colonizers, to India, New Zealand, Australia, mainland Europe, South Africa, South America and the USA. The first golf club in America was established in 1888. Situated at Yonkers on the east coast, it was appropriately called St Andrews. America's first 18-hole golf course, Shinnecock Hills, also on the east coast, opened in 1891 and, in 1896, it hosted the second ever US Open.

In the winter of 1889, William K Vanderbilt, son of the founder of the Vanderbilt empire, was visiting France where he met Scotsman Willie Dunn Jr, professional and course designer at Biarritz and former professional at Westward Ho! in England. Vanderbilt took a fancy to the game and, on returning to the USA, he began planning the construction of a golf course at the summer resort of Southampton on Long Island. Recruited to build the course, Dunn found the terrain to be ideal. Close to the Atlantic Ocean and exposed to the prevailing winds, with sandy, rolling hills and long, coarse grass, it resembled a piece of classic Scottish linksland.

With the help of 150 Native Americans from the Shinnecock tribe which occupied the far end of the island, Dunn completed 12 holes by 1891. A top architect of the time, Stanford White, was called in to build the stately clubhouse that still presides over the surrounding countryside today, and is the oldest in the USA.

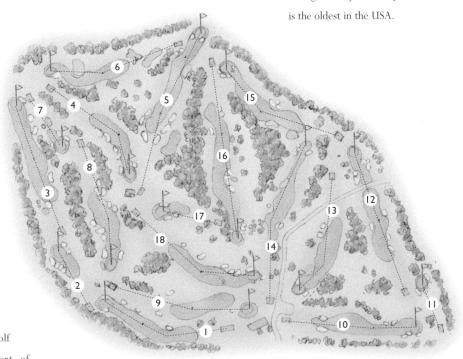

LEFT: *Large bunkers line the approach to the par-five 16th at Shinnecock Hills. In the course's early days it was not unusual for players to encounter strange objects such as human bones when playing bunker shots, as the course covers burial grounds of the ancients.*

In 1892, Dunn completed the remaining six holes, and the 18-hole layout quickly developed a large following among Southampton's wealthy summer residents, becoming the first golf club in the USA with a membership waiting list. In the early years, members played in red jackets in remembrance and imitation of the British tradition – to warn passers-by that golfers were present.

Although Shinnecock hosted the US Amateur and the US Open in 1896, and the US Women's Amateur in 1900, it measured only 4572m (5000yd) and was not considered long enough for championship golf. In 1931, Dick Wilson expanded the layout to its current championship length of 6349m (6944yd). Although this is still considered short by today's standards, the par-70 layout utilizes the effect of the prevailing southwest winds, with many par threes and short par fours playing into the teeth of the wind.

The course regained its Major status in 1986, hosting its second US Open a full 90 years after hosting its first Major. Although three players broke the course record of 68 by three strokes that year, they were tested by the narrow, undulating fairways bordered by long grass, and by the extensive bunkering. The event was won by American Ray Floyd with a score of one under par (279).

When American Corey Pavin won the 1995 US Open at Shinnecock, it was with a score of level par (280). The layout should again prove to be a worthy challenge in the 2004 US Open to be held there.

Shinnecock Hill's opening hole, the par-four 1st, is named Westward Ho! after the course in England where Scottish designer Willie Dunn had served as a professional before going to the USA, but it is Shinnecock's par-four 18th hole that is perhaps most reminiscent of a Scottish links, with its undulating fairway and dense rough on either side. The wind from the right makes it difficult to keep the ball on the fairway and the long approach shot must clear the two bunkers guarding the front of the green. The hole provides a fitting close to a challenging and varied golf course.

ABOVE RIGHT: *Shinnecock Hills' par-three 17th is played over thick Fescue grass to a green flanked by several bunkers.*

SHINNECOCK HILLS
GARY PLAYER'S VIEW

The USA's first great golf course, Shinnecock Hills, is a work of art with a heart and soul all its own. Not technically a links course since it does not literally buttress up against the sea, it nonetheless feels and plays like one, requiring demanding approach shots to all the greens. Each hole presents a different, demanding yet fair challenge, requiring a well-rounded game. Playing at this great course has been among the most memorable golf experiences of my life, and, of course, the Long Island sunsets over the bay in mid-summer are hard to beat.

RASPBERRY FALLS

Golf and hunting on Raspberry Plain

LEESBURG, VIRGINIA, USA

The state of Virginia, near Washington DC in the eastern USA, is a most unlikely place to find a Scottish links-style golf course. However, a mere 15-minute drive northwest from Washington's Dulles airport, near Leesburg, Virginia, lies the Raspberry Falls Golf and Hunt Club. Opened in October 1996, it is a Gary Player Design creation and the only Gary Player Signature Course in the state of Virginia.

The 6575m (7191yd) par-72 Raspberry Falls layout rambles across Raspberry Plain, an area established in the 18th century as an exceptionally productive and fertile plantation. While the Raspberry Falls landscape, with its rocky outcrops, rolling grasslands, tall hardwood trees and meandering streams, is not typical links land, the terrain has a links-like openness with excellent vistas. Perhaps with this in mind, a number of links-style features have been incorporated into the design, including deep Scottish-style pot bunkers with steep, stacked-sod walls that are a design feature much favoured by Player.

The British Isles theme is continued in the 'Hunt Club' decor of the impressive Southern-mansion-style clubhouse and the traditional hunt-master dress worn by the attendants. Fox hunting, an age-old pastime in the British Isles, has recently become popular amongst the equestrian community in northern Virginia, and Raspberry Falls hosts visits from the Loudoun Hunt West fox-hunting club in autumn, winter and early spring. The golf course and surrounds offer a perfect setting for a hunt with lush pastures, stone walls, hedges and streams. Golfers out for a quiet round may find themselves treated to the unusual sight of a fox hunt in full flight, with the horses and pack taking advantage of the course's 'hunt crossings'.

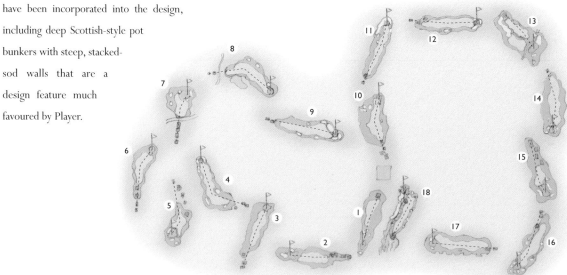

RIGHT: *The open, rolling terrain of Raspberry Plain proved to be an ideal site for Gary Player to construct a Scottish links-style golf course. The Southern-mansion-style clubhouse is also home to the Loudoun Hunt West fox-hunting club.*

As Gary Player himself comments, 'Raspberry Falls is like nothing you have ever experienced this side of the Atlantic. Although it does not enjoy tournament status, it is a public golf course that allows all who make the effort to get there to enjoy the experience'.

RASPBERRY FALLS
GARY PLAYER'S VIEW

This is one of my favourite public golf courses, and I enjoyed designing it. It is what is today called an 'upscale daily fee' facility, so players receive the kind of attention and service they would at an exclusive country club. Knowledge of contemporary golf course architecture and state-of-the-art building equipment made it possible for Raspberry Falls to replicate a traditional Scottish links-style course. Few Americans will have seen the kind of stacked-sod bunkers they find here, inspired as they are by the great seaside courses of the British Isles.

SEMINOLE

A Donald Ross classic

NORTH PALM BEACH, FLORIDA, USA

As the game of golf boomed throughout the USA in the 1920s, the era became known as the Golden Age of golf course architecture. In 1929, the great Donald Ross created Seminole Golf Club on the coast of Florida. Born in 1872 in Dornoch, Scotland, Ross was later appointed as professional and greenkeeper on one of the country's great links courses, Royal Dornoch. After emigrating to the USA in 1899, he worked at the famous Pinehurst golf resort in Massachusetts where he was to remain as director of golf until his death in 1948.

Raised on linksland courses, Ross incorporated many Scottish-style features into his layouts. This is apparent in the open, links-like landscape at Seminole, which has extensive bunkering and many water hazards, while the natural contours of the land have been left in place and trees are scarce.

Although significant modifications were made by Dick Wilson in 1947, and again by Ed Connor in 1991, the course retains its distinctive Ross character. Many holes at Seminole are designed to play alongside the ocean, including the signature hole, the 381m (417 yd) par-four 18th. The terrain is mostly flat, although most of the tees and undulating Tifdwarf grass greens are slightly elevated, and a ridge of mounding comes into play in the middle of the golf course.

Florida is a golfer's paradise with a vast number of golf courses, so it is some commendation for Seminole to be rated as the top course in the state for four years running, as it was by *Golf Digest* from 1995 to 1998. This 18-hole, par-72 course, playing to 6206m (6787yd) and rated 73.6 off the back tees, was also ranked 4th on *Golfweek*'s list of America's 10 Best Classical Courses for 1999.

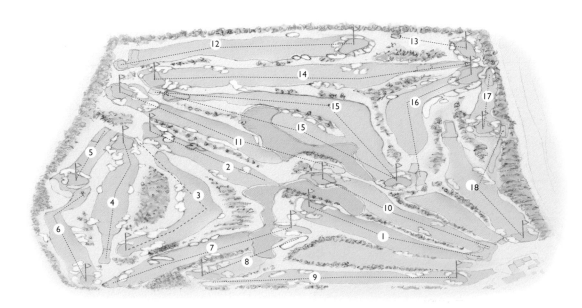

RIGHT: *This aerial view of Seminole's clubhouse and busy practice green and driving range also shows the course's open, links-like terrain and the effect of the strong sea breeze. The course's signature hole is the par-four 18th that borders the ocean.*

SEMINOLE
GARY PLAYER'S VIEW

This is the first golf course I played in the USA and also where I had my first round of golf with Ben Hogan. Indeed, Hogan was a member and loved playing and practising here. He once said: 'If you can play Seminole, you can play any course in the world.' The course is built along the sand dunes next to the ocean, and requires precise placement off the tee. It has great atmosphere, a variety of beautiful and sternly bunkered greens, and is always in wonderful condition. Known for its hospitality, Seminole's locker room is the most fabulous into which I have ever ventured.

ABOVE: *Seminole features extensive bunkering, as is apparent in this view of the par-three 13th hole.*

ABOVE: *The par-four 7th at the Links at Fancourt. The flat farmland on which the course was built was once used as an airstrip. Through the use of heavy duty earth-moving machinery, the Gary Player Design Group moved more than 700,000 metric tonnes of clay to create the natural-looking mounds and wetland features reminiscent of the great links courses of Scotland and Ireland. In describing the course, Gary Player has been quoted as saying, 'I knew this was going to take some imagination and I think we've come up with something that is a masterpiece.'*

THE LINKS AT FANCOURT
GARY PLAYER'S VIEW

I feel this is one of the very best golf courses in the world, even though it may have been built on the worst piece of ground – clay as flat as an airport. I'm proud to have worked as the course designer and could not be happier with how it turned out. It has been designed to make golfers feel as though they were at Ballybunion, Dornoch, or St Andrews with rolling fairways, pot bunkers, big greens, high rough, and a seascape appearance.

THE LINKS AT FANCOURT

Toughest test in South Africa

GEORGE, SOUTH AFRICA

Fancourt Hotel and Country Club Estate in the small town of George is some 400km (250 miles) from Cape Town. Built as one of South Africa's first estate-type golf facilities in the early 1980s, it was saved from financial difficulties by German software magnate Hasso Plattner in the mid-1990s. Sparing no expense, Plattner commissioned a second course as well as a four-hole academy course and golf school, creating one of the finest estates in Southern Africa.

He then approached Gary Player, who had designed and constructed the first two courses, inviting him to construct a third world-class course – with a request this time to incorporate links-like characteristics.

Having studied courses such as Ballybunion in Ireland and other links courses in Scotland, Gary Player Design created a masterpiece on what had once been an airfield and later a dumping ground. Thousands of tonnes of clay were bulldozed to construct mounds on the flat ground to achieve the links-like effect.

The course has been designed to be the toughest test of golf in South Africa. As Gary Player has commented, golfers will realize that 'this game ain't meant to be fair!' Long and difficult, it is exposed to the winds that funnel through the impressive surrounding Outeniqua mountains and combines all the features of the best links courses of Scotland and Ireland: the long, secluded walks on fairways set between massive dunes; the waving Rye and Fescue grasses in the rough; and the blind and semi-blind tee shots and approach shots to large, undulating greens. Wetlands similar to those found on genuine linksland in the coastal regions of Scotland and Ireland have been constructed to add to the authenticity of the experience so that golfers in Africa can, as Gary Player desires, 'experience their very own British Open'.

Opened for play in November 2000, The Links at Fancourt is the only one of Fancourt's four courses open to non-members and non-residents of the estate or hotel. With the course hosting the President's Cup in 2002, it will certainly be tested by the world's best professionals.

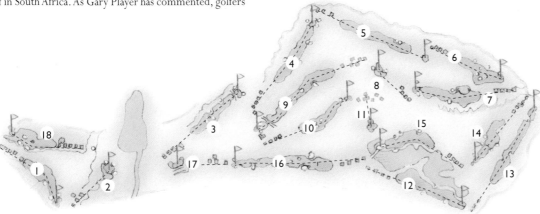

RIGHT: *The approach to the par-four 3rd at the Links at Fancourt must be long enough to avoid the steep, banked 'burn-like' water hazard that crosses the fairway at the front of the green, another typical links-like feature incorporated into the Fancourt layout.*

NOORDWIJK

GARY PLAYER'S VIEW

This top-notch golf course has hosted several Dutch Opens, an important national championship with a long history. The course combines links and parkland features in a challenging yet fair test of golf. It has an ample selection of tees to accommodate the playing ability of a wide range of golfers. It winds through sand dunes and along the sea, but also presents four inland wooded holes — an unusual blend that calls to mind a great golf course such as Spyglass Hill on California's Monterey Peninsula. When the winds kick up, Noordwijk, like all classic links layouts, really gets tough. True to the characteristic of links golf, this course will thoroughly challenge all of one's skills.

ABOVE: *The clubhouse at Noordwijkse Golf Club looks out over the green of the 9th hole.*

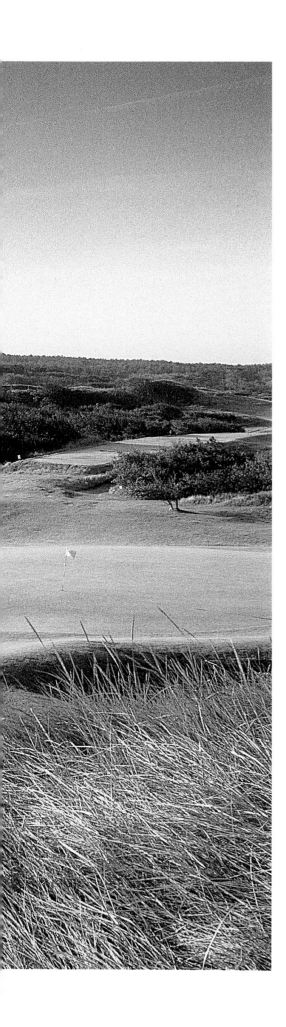

NOORDWIJK

A Dutch masterpiece

NOORDWIJK, NETHERLANDS

The Noordwijkse Golf Club celebrated its 85th birthday in 1999, the year in which it hosted the 81st Dutch Open. The course on which this event was played, however, is slightly younger. In 1971 the old nine-hole course gave way to the expansion of the village of Noordwijk and the golf club was moved several kilometres to the north, where there was room for 18 holes and three practice holes. The layout at this location has rapidly built up an international reputation and established itself on the European championship roster. Exceptional patience is required to conquer this devilish course. Its typically links-like landscape of rolling dunes alongside the North Sea is made considerably tougher by the prevailing southwesterly wind. Designed by British golf course architect, Frank Pennink, the 6291m (6880yd), par-72 layout has hosted the Dutch Open Championship nine times since 1978. Australian Stephen Leaney took the 2000 title with a 19-under-par score of 269. Spaniard Seve Ballesteros's victory in the Dutch Open played at Noordwijk in 1986 was remarkable for several reasons. He won by a runaway eight strokes, the same margin by which he won his first professional event – the Dutch Open at nearby Kennemer Golf Club – 10 years earlier. (Payne Stewart bettered this finish

by recording a nine-stroke victory the next time the event was played at Noordwijk in 1991.) Ballesteros's win in 1986 also made him the first European golfer to accumulate more than £1 million in prize money.

The 1986 event was, however, marred by the gouging of deep holes in the 3rd and 11th greens by anti-apartheid demonstrators, forcing PGA European Tour officials to take them out of play for one round. The record books show that Ballesteros's score of 271 was set over only 70 holes.

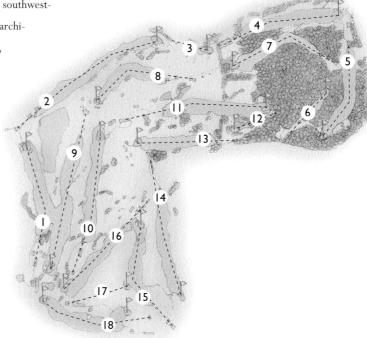

LEFT: *The rolling dunes, open terrain and thick rough typical of links golf courses are apparent in this view of Noordwijk's 15th hole. The Dutch Open, traditionally played the week after the Open Championship, has been played at Noordwijk on nine occasions.*

SAND RIVER
Palm-enhanced links style

SHENZHEN BAY, CHINA

Located in Shenzhen province, a 15-minute drive from the boundary of Hong Kong, where the river meets the South China Sea at Shenzhen Bay, the Gary Player-designed Sand River Golf Club has a 'very British links-like feel'. Perhaps this has much to do with the ever-present breeze that can cause havoc with golfers' scores, sometimes turning fairly easy-looking par fours into embarrassingly long monsters.

There are perhaps fewer bunkers around the course than would be expected on a genuine links course, rather more expansive in their shape than the traditional small pot bunkers. Many of the greens have the extra defence of raised areas guarding their entrance, but these generally feed down to the greens in traditional links style. The liberal use of water as a design feature adds to the relative difficulty of the course.

Unlike a true links course, the fairways tend to hold the ball rather than promoting the extensive run associated with some of the better-known links courses of Britain and Ireland. Possibly the most anomalous feature of this 18-hole facility are its numerous palm trees – perhaps a reminder to the purist that the course is meant only to have links-like characteristics without pretending to be something it is not.

In addition to the 18-hole facility there is a nine-hole floodlit course, as well as a Gary Player teaching facility, tennis courts, function rooms, a restaurant and even a karaoke lounge.

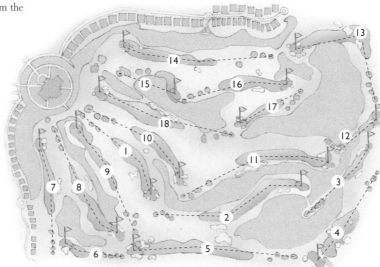

SAND RIVER
GARY PLAYER'S VIEW

My design team and I built part of this golf course on land that was reclaimed from the South China Sea. It is a beautiful links-style layout with 27 holes and a great teaching facility. Golfers in China are improving at a rapid rate, and this course should help that country rise in status in the eyes of world golf.

RIGHT, TOP AND BOTTOM: *The links-like mounds and bunkers of Sand River's 18-hole course almost mirror the backdrop of the mountains of Hong Kong. As the palm trees grow they will afford some shelter from the winds blowing in off the South China Sea.*

KAU SAI CHAU

The 'St Andrews' of Hong Kong

THE JOCKEY CLUB, KAU SAI CHAU PUBLIC GOLF CLUB, HONG KONG

Opened in 1995, the Kau Sai Chau Golf Course is one of only two public golf facilities in land-starved Hong Kong. In fact, there are two courses – North and South – in a picturesque and tranquil setting on the northern end of Kau Sai Chau Island, with magnificent views of the Sai Kung hills on mainland Hong Kong.

Not surprisingly, neither of the Gary Player-designed courses is particularly long, and the greens and tees are fairly close to one another. As with most links-like courses, the winds off the surrounding sea play a dominant role, substantially increasing the difficulty of both courses when they are at their fiercest.

The North course has several spectacular holes, including the par-three 3rd which is played across a water inlet to a steeply banked green. The undulating green means that even if a golfer successfully negotiates the 157m (172yd) distance, par is not a certainty.

The tee shot on the 425m (465yd) par-four 9th is across water to a wide plateau from which a long-iron is required to reach the green – and then only once the gusting winds that blow through a narrow valley at the rear of the green have been negotiated.

The par-four 15th is interesting for its walled fairway that creates a sheer drop on the left-hand side. The valley below is a breeding ground for a unique species of insects that were left undisturbed by the construction of the golf courses. The hole

also has a panoramic view of the course, the imposing clubhouse and the sea in the distance. The par-five 17th makes use of a number of bunkers up the right-hand side of the fairway to force the tee shot to the left, a theme that is repeated all the way up to the green.

On the South course, the very short par-three 16th makes ingenious use of grass bunkers filled with waving Zoysia grass, requiring an accurate tee shot on a hole measuring just 98m (107yd).

Accessible by ferry from Sai Kung harbour, the course is open to anyone with an official handicap. There is also a 72-bay driving range and an academy, as well as several restaurants and other facilities like mini-golf.

KAU SAI CHAU
GARY PLAYER'S VIEW

The British Navy once used the land on which the North and South courses now stand as a target practice artillery site, and it was badly scarred by erosion. Today, with their natural beauty, these 36 holes rival any public golf course in the world. In fact, although it is a public facility, some golf course rating experts have spoken of Kau Sai Chau in the same breath as St Andrews and Pebble Beach – a view that really pleases the golf course architect part of me. For challenging holes and scenic beauty as you play alongside and across the South China Sea, it does not get much better than the North course.

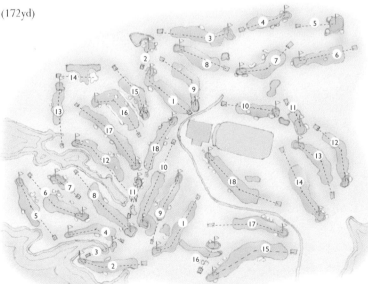

LEFT AND ABOVE RIGHT: *The two 18-hole golf courses built on a former naval shooting range at Kau Sai Chau both feature typical links-like characteristics – wide open rolling fairways, punishing rough and bunkers, and few, if any, trees.*

PARKLAND GOLF COURSES

Shaped by man and machine

A NATURAL PROGRESSION IN THE EVOLUTION OF THE game was for golf courses eventually to move away from coastal linksland and be laid out on inland areas. Today, the vast majority of the world's golf courses are situated inland and most of these are 'parkland' in nature.

This descriptive term implies a course that has a park-like atmosphere, characterized by an abundance of trees, shrubbery and other attractive natural features such as lakes and streams. A key factor determining the status of a parkland course is its 'maturity' – tall trees lining the fairways, prominent water features and streams, and thick undergrowth alongside the playing corridor make the course appear established and 'mature'.

The secret of success on parkland courses is what is referred to in the golfing world as 'target' or 'dartboard' golf. While golfers will frequently run the ball along the ground to the green on links courses, approach shots on parkland courses are generally played through the air. And, while the greens on links courses are generally hard, those on parkland courses are often soft and receptive, meaning that a well-struck shot will stop quickly on impact. It is interesting to note that while most links courses have the same type of grass cover from tee to green, parkland courses generally have a variety of grasses, with Bermuda fairways and Bent grass greens being common species.

Because of the well-wooded nature of many parkland courses, longer shots often have to be 'shaped' through the air. It is less important to be able to hit the ball high or low in parkland environments, but the ability to draw or fade the ball is a major advantage.

Parkland courses can be classified into two broad categories: classical and modern. Older parkland courses, designed before World War II, are generally regarded as classics, while

younger courses are referred to as modern layouts. In recent years, many classic layouts have been modernized through the reconstruction and enlargement of bunkers and greens. Close attention is paid, however, to preserving their classic characteristics and atmosphere. Modern parkland courses often have 'novelty' features such as railroad sleepers in bunkers and large water features specifically placed on the course to serve as hazards.

Given the fact that most of the world's courses fall into the parkland category, it comes as no surprise that the majority of high-profile golf tournaments are staged on parkland layouts. Although the British Open is played only on links courses, more Major championships have been decided on parkland layouts than on any other type.

The US Open is virtually always played on parkland layouts and even a course such as Pebble Beach, where Tiger Woods shattered a host of records during the 2000 event, has numerous parkland features and holes despite its status as an ocean course. Other notable parkland layouts that have hosted the US Open include Winged Foot in New York, Congressional in Washington, Oakmont in Pennsylvania and Pinehurst in North Carolina, while one of the most famous parkland layouts in the United Kingdom – Wentworth in England – has been home to the World Matchplay Championship for over three decades.

Two of the top three courses in the USA (as ranked by American publication *Golfweek* in 2000), Pine Valley and Augusta National, are parkland layouts, and Augusta's status as the home of the Masters has made it the world's most famous and televised golf course. Gary Player once commented: 'If there is a golf course in heaven, I hope it is like Augusta National. I just do not want an early tee time!'

ABOVE: *The 10th hole at Valderrama in Sotogrande, Spain, is typical of a parkland course with its established trees guarding the driving area and a man-made water hazard protecting the approach to the green. In 1997, the course was the venue for the first European continental hosting of the biennial Ryder Cup matches between professionals from the USA and Europe.*

ABOVE: *Measuring 425m (465yd), the 5th hole at Oakland Hills is a long par four with typical parkland features such as lush fairways, tall trees and a stream crossing the playing area. This famous course has hosted the US Open Championship on no fewer than six occasions between 1924 and 1996, the year when American Steve Jones won his first Major with a four-round total of 278.*

AUGUSTA NATIONAL

Bobby Jones' vision

AUGUSTA, GEORGIA, USA

Arguably the most famous and exclusive golf club in the USA, Augusta National was the brainchild of legendary amateur golfer Bobby Jones, who in 1930 uniquely won the Open and Amateur Championships of the USA and Britain.

Together with his friend and business associate, Clifford Roberts, Jones selected the land (then the Fruitlands Nurseries) on which he dreamt of building a top quality golf course of national renown. Despite the recent stock market crash and subsequent Depression, they found finance for their venture from wealthy businessmen who had survived the economic woes of the time. In 1933, some 80 founder members of Augusta National assembled, and Jones and Roberts were unanimously voted in as president and chairman respectively.

The course itself was designed by Dr Alister Mackenzie in consultation with Jones, and was formally opened in December 1932, just a month before the club was officially opened.

In 1934, the Masters tournament, originally known as the Augusta National Invitational Tournament, was first played here. It was not until the following year when Gene Sarazen hit the 'shot that was heard around the world' – the four-wood to score a two on the par-five 15th – that the tournament began to capture the imagination of the world's golfers.

Since then the course that is famed for its absolute perfection in terms of conditioning has become the benchmark against which all parkland courses around the world are measured.

Each immaculate hole has a remarkable history, but it is possibly 'Amen Corner' (referring to holes 11, 12 and 13) that is most famous – the scene of many a change in fortunes come the Sunday of the Masters tournament. As the pressure of the final nine holes mounts, many a golfer has seen his dreams shattered as his ball finds the ubiquitous and notorious Rae's Creek.

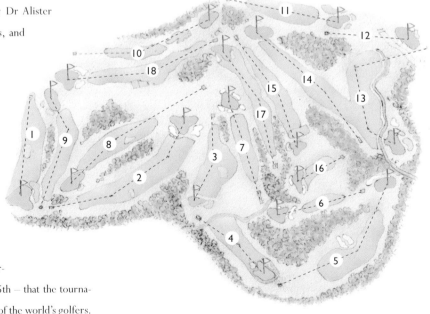

LEFT: *Before golfers hit the notorious Amen Corner at Augusta National, they play the 443m (485yd) 10th hole, one of the longest par fours in Major championship play. The 10th starts the second nine with a downhill drive from the tee situated near the clubhouse.*

The clubhouse, built in 1854 by the owner of the then indigo plantation, Dennis Redman, is considered to be the first cement construction in the southern USA. The 230m (250yd) drive up to the clubhouse, known as Magnolia Lane, is probably as famous as the course itself, boasting 60 magnolia trees planted in the late 1850s. The course regularly undergoes slight design changes (or 'improvements', as the committee would have it) that include the growing of semi-rough and the slight lengthening of holes, keeping abreast of advances in the modern game.

AUGUSTA NATIONAL

GARY PLAYER'S VIEW

Augusta National is one of my three favourite golf courses in the world, along with Cypress Point and The Links at Fancourt. Hosting the Masters every year, it really begins the golfing season in the USA. It is particularly beautiful when the dogwoods and azaleas are in bloom in early April. To have won this Major tournament three times is special. People still ask me which Masters victory I cherish most, but that is like asking a proud parent of three which child he loves the most.

ABOVE LEFT: *Tom Watson helps Gary Player don the green jacket after he won the 1978 Masters at Augusta, having shot 64 in the final which included a back nine completed in just 30 shots. At the age of 42, Player was then the oldest player to have won the Masters. In 1986, Jack Nicklaus surpassed Player's record by winning at the age of 46.*

ABOVE: *Reconstructed in 1947, the par-three 16th at Augusta demands an accurate tee shot played entirely over water to the green, which slopes significantly from right to left.*

RIGHT: *Known as the Flowering Crab Apple, the long par-three 4th is often made difficult by deceptive wind, which makes it tough to reach the flag on the boomerang-shaped green.*

COUGAR POINT

A marshland masterpiece

KIAWAH ISLAND RESORT, KIAWAH ISLAND, SOUTH CAROLINA, USA

Kiawah Island, a strip of land 16km (10 miles) wide, off the coast of South Carolina in the USA, is rich in meandering lagoons and pristine marshlands. Bordered by the Atlantic Ocean to the south and the Kiawah River to the north, it is home to five exceptional golf courses.

The list of designers at Kiawah Island Resort reads like a who's who of modern golf course architecture: Pete Dye, Tom Fazio, Clyde Johnston, Jack Nicklaus and Gary Player – all names with a familiar ring – have each created a championship golf course in varied terrain of sandy dunes and forests of pine, oak and palm trees. The resultant collection of golf courses – Oak Point, Cougar Point, Turtle Point, Osprey Point and the Ocean Course – is as diverse as the architects themselves.

Cougar Point is Gary Player's creation on Kiawah Island, a 5792m (6334yd), par-71 layout featuring holes playing directly along broad expanses of tidal marsh and offering panoramic views of the Kiawah River and acres of needlerush and Spartina grass. Situated at the western edge of Kiawah Island, between West Beach Village and the river, the course meanders through the island's marshlands where water is a prominent feature. In all, 13 holes have water hazards. Although the course is relatively short, it has small, undulating Tifdwarf Bermuda grass greens and its narrow fairways demand accurate shot placement. Cougar Point presents a challenge to the serious golfer, but the range of tee options allows even those with a high handicap to enjoy a social round.

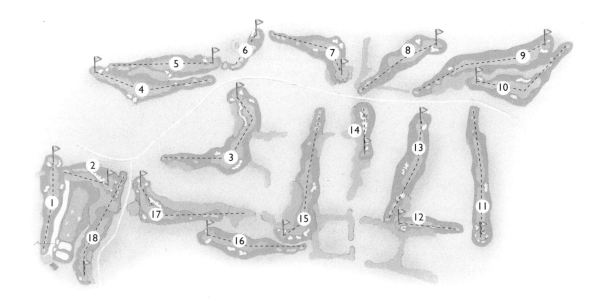

LEFT: *The green of the 5th hole at Cougar Point is situated on a raised peninsula surrounded by tidal marshland, with the Kiawah River visible in the background. Gary Player is one of five modern golf course architects to have created a championship course on Kiawah Island.*

COUGAR POINT

GARY PLAYER'S VIEW

I knew that as there are so many golf courses on Kiawah Island, my design team and I would have to create something special if we were to add another — and I think we have. Depending on the tees played, it will challenge the scratch golfer and the resort player. Kiawah Island is a paradise for golf, with Cougar Point located right on the ocean. It is a course that you can play again and again, as there is always something new to discover, both on the golf course itself and among the variety of natural life to which the course is home.

ABOVE LEFT: *Appropriately in an area of lagoons and marshland, water comes into play on no less than 13 of the holes at Cougar Point, including the 17th, where Palmetto Palm trees line the back of the heavily bunkered green.*

ABOVE RIGHT: *Tall pines, oaks and palms line the fairways at Cougar Point, meandering through acres of waterways and swampland on the western part of Kiawah Island.*

DIAMOND RUN

Diamond in the rough

SEWICKLEY, PENNSYLVANIA, USA

Diamond Run Golf Club is living proof that, with a little planning and effort, golf courses and homes can exist happily together. Diamond Run combines a superb 18-hole golf course with a well-positioned, unobtrusive residential estate. It also features a Gary Player Signature Course – a layout in which Gary had hands-on involvement in both design and construction – which winds through rolling landscape and scenic wooded areas.

Measuring 6331m (6924yd) when played off the championship tees, the course was built in 1992 as a private course for a select group of founding shareholders. The club opened officially in 1994 and by 1998 membership had grown to 300 despite initiation fees of up to US$27,000. In 1998, after winning a membership vote by 177 to 20, Diamond Run's owners and founding members sold the small and exclusive club to Club Corp, one of the largest golf course operators in the USA. The owners walked away with US$10.6 million while the club's members acquired all the benefits of belonging to a large conglomerate, including access to over 200 clubs and resorts around the country.

Gary Player's hand is evident everywhere in the design of this course, which features wide, undulating fairways with long, defined cuts of rough and greens that are soft enough to hold a shot. The signature hole is the spectacular 16th, a 384m (420yd) par four that requires a tee shot from an elevated box. A huge ravine runs along the entire left side of the dogleg left fairway, while large boulders behind the green spell trouble for the golfer who overclubs his approach shot. Water hazards come into play on 10 of the holes, including three that require a shot over water.

Diamond Run's real estate development takes up 130ha (321 acres), while the 18-hole golf course occupies all of 200ha (494 acres), which helps to create a quiet, natural setting in which golfers can enjoy this excellent course.

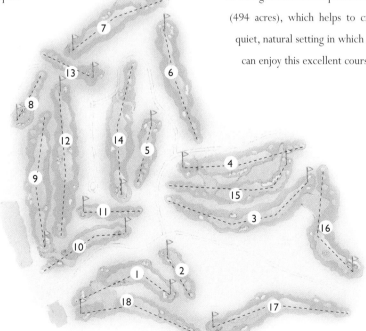

LEFT AND ABOVE RIGHT: *The Gary Player-designed Diamond Run Golf Club in Sewickley, Pennsylvania, is laid out over a dramatically undulating landscape, featuring beautifully wooded areas and a relatively unobtrusive and exclusive housing estate.*

DIAMOND RUN
GARY PLAYER'S VIEW

This is probably the best real estate housing development golf course I have seen or designed. The houses are high above the fairways so golfers do not feel as though they are playing in a residential neighbourhood, yet residents can enjoy a beautiful view of the golf course below their homes. The clubhouse is situated high on a hill and also offers great vistas. Most greens are built in an amphitheatre-like setting, guarded by trees and bunkers.

INVERNESS

Home of the 'Hinkle Tree'

TOLEDO, OHIO, USA

Professional golfers today are respected members of the golfing community, admired both for their ability on the golf course and for the standard of dress and decorum that has come to be associated with those in the paid ranks. However, in the early part of the 20th century, strong class distinction existed between elite, generally wealthy amateur golfers and professionals. This outdated tradition came to an end at the 1920 US Open at Inverness Club in Toledo, Ohio, when, for the first time, professional golfers were invited into the clubhouse, allowed access to the locker room and restaurant, and permitted to use the front door of the club. Inverness club president JP Jermain's gesture of hospitality was well received by the pros, particularly by two-time US Open winner Walter Hagen who presented the club with a chiming clock inscribed with the words:

'God measures men by what they are
Not what they in wealth possess
That vibrant message chimes afar
The voice of Inverness.'

Pipe-smoking Englishman, Ted Ray, won the US Open that year, the first time the event had been staged at Inverness.

Although the club opened in 1903, when nine holes were laid out through the wooded, gently undulating landscape, it was only in 1919, after 18 new holes were designed by renowned Scottish golf course architect, Donald Ross, that it was elevated to championship status. Inverness hosted the US Open on three subsequent occasions, in 1931, 1957 and 1979, with modifications being made to the course before each event, first by AW Tillinghast, later by Dick Wilson, and finally by George Fazio. Inverness also hosted the US PGA Championship in 1986 and 1993, but it is for two particular incidents in its Major championship history that it is best remembered.

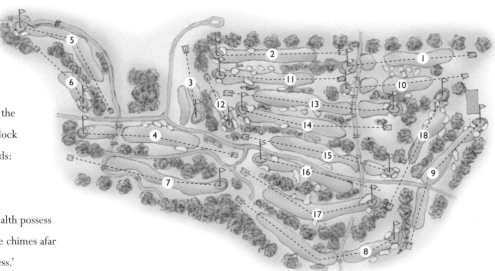

RIGHT: *Inverness' par-four 5th green is surrounded by large sand traps. Extensive bunkering and lightning-fast greens characterize the Inverness layout, while, in typical parkland style, tall trees line the gently undulating fairways.*

During the first round of the 1979 US Open, Lon Hinkle discovered a short cut to the green of the par-five 8th, the longest hole on the course measuring all of 483m (528yd). Hinkle's 'alternative route' involved deliberately hitting his ball off the tee onto the fairway of the adjacent 17th hole, from where he proceeded to birdie the 8th after knocking a full 55m (60yd) off its length. The organizers of the US Open, the US Golf Association, were so perturbed that, to the astonishment of the players, they planted a tall pine tree overnight, alongside the 8th tee to block the short cut. It measured 7m (24ft) in height and was 5m (16ft) wide at its base. Undeterred, Hinkle hit the ball over the tree and it became affectionately known as the 'Hinkle Tree'. That

year the US Open was won by Hale Irwin, his second victory in the event. Behind him was 1965 US Open champion, Gary Player, who finished as runner-up in the event for the second time.

Inverness is a challenging golf course renowned for its lightning-fast greens and extensive bunkering: 110 sand traps dot the fairways and protect the greens. It was not until the 1986 US PGA Championship that par was broken in a four-day tournament over the 6284m (6982yd) layout.

That year, Bob Tway scored an eight-under-par total of 276 to record his first and only Major victory, but his performance is remembered for one superb shot. Measuring only 324m (354yd), the 18th is the course's shortest par

four, but the small green is well protected front and left by several sand traps. Tway's approach shot found the bunker in front of the green, but his recovery shot landed softly on the green and rolled into the cup for birdie, giving him victory over Greg Norman. Coincidentally, Norman was again denied victory when Inverness hosted the 1993 US PGA Championship, with Paul Azinger defeating the Australian in a playoff to claim his only Major title.

Although Inverness has only three par threes and two par fives, which is unusual for a course chosen to host the US Open, the par-71 layout is rated 74.3 and, as a test of skill, it provides a fitting venue for the national championship of one of the world's great golfing nations.

INVERNESS
GARY PLAYER'S VIEW

This is a rolling course with trees, brooks, plenty of bunkers and undulating greens where the straight hitter really has an advantage. Particularly good bunkering and superb tee construction for both men and women make this a great golf course.

ABOVE LEFT: *Two narrow streams are prominent in the defences of many holes at Inverness, guarding a number of greens uncompromisingly.*

ABOVE: *Golfers make their way towards the final green from Inverness' 18th tee. Although this par four measures only 323m (354yd), designer Donald Ross laid several traps in front of, and to the left of, the small green to snare imprecise shots.*

MANHATTAN WOODS

Tranquil and unspoilt

ROCKLANDS COUNTY, NEW YORK, USA

Manhattan Woods Golf Club in West Nyack, Rocklands County, is easily accessible from Manhattan, northern New Jersey, Westchester and lower Connecticut.

With its idyllic woodland layout, it is the first course designed by Gary Player in the New York region, and opened for play in September 1998. The tranquil 6492m (7100yd) course is laid out over gently sloping terrain offering views of Manhattan from several holes. The playability of the course is enhanced through the use of a variety of tee boxes and therefore differing hole lengths, which allows golfers of all levels of skill to be tested fairly.

'I know this is a tall order, but I want to make Manhattan Woods one of the top five golf courses in the metropolitan area,' said Ken Lee, owner of the course. 'I have kept the land in its natural form and resisted spoiling it with hundreds of homesits, wanting to preserve the property as a tranquil garden to be enjoyed by members.' With this in mind, Lee has restricted the resident membership to an invited 240, with another 40 nonresidents and 100 social members who enjoy the facilities of the clubhouse.

Gary Player believes that Manhattan Woods will be a haven for members who work in New York City. 'Our goal at Manhattan Woods was to create an environment for people to relax and enjoy. Take time out to view the skyline of Manhattan from various points on the course and compare your state of mind to that when you are in traffic or at the office. I believe you will come to realize that the beauty of nature truly has a soothing effect on the soul.'

This young 18-hole course, blended with streams and wetlands, has the potential to become one of the finest parkland courses in a region famous for examples such as Winged Foot, Westchester and Oak Hill, all of which have hosted important events on the US PGA Tour.

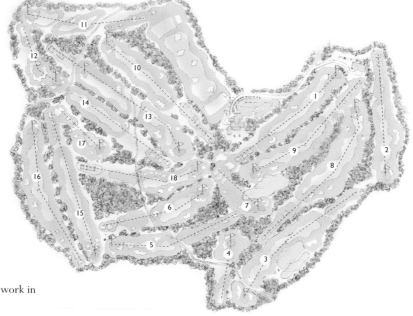

RIGHT: *Manhattan Woods, Gary Player's first golf course design project in the New York region, opened for play in September 1998. Constructed on undulating terrain, the tree-lined fairways offer views of nearby metropolitan Manhattan from several points on the course.*

ABOVE: *The attractive Manhattan Woods layout, although still a young course, has already hosted the Karrie Webb Celebrity Pro-Am, an event in aid of the well-known actor Christopher Reeves' Paralysis Foundation. It will soon be added to the roster of courses that host events on the US Senior Tour.*

MANHATTAN WOODS
GARY PLAYER'S VIEW

As the first course I have designed in the New York City area, I wanted Manhattan Woods, a private club, to pay homage to the worldwide importance and excitement of this great metropolis. While you can see the famous sky-line of Manhattan from the golf course, you certainly cannot feel New York City's equally talked-about stress. On a tranquil and naturally beautiful stretch of land, Manhattan Woods is already a wonderful challenge with its undulating and tree-lined fairways; as this young course matures, it should grow in stature.

MEDINAH

Long and unforgiving

NO. 3 COURSE, MEDINAH, ILLINOIS, USA

Situated in a suburb of Chicago, Medinah was built in the 1920s for the Ancient Arabic Order of Nobles of the Mystic Shrine, a society known for its charitable works.

Scottish architect Tom Bendelow was commissioned to lay out 54 holes on the 263ha (650 acres) of land west of Lake Michigan and, interestingly, the now-famous Course No. 3 was originally constructed as the ladies' course. At just 5683m (6215yd) it was a far cry from today's extent of more than 6766m (7400yd).

The course was ultimately considered too difficult for ladies and was handed over to the men. When the 1930 US Open was played there, Harry Cooper roared through the final round on his way to a 63 and the title, more than a little irritating the members. As a result, five new holes were laid out to toughen it up and prevent similar feats in future.

Besides the length of Medinah, some 4200 trees make for a very unforgiving layout, placing a premium on exceptionally accurate driving of the ball. The course is laid out on 85ha (205 acres) of land, with only 12ha (30 acres) taken up by fairway. Add to this the notorious winds that whip off the lakes surrounding Chicago and it is no wonder that the USGA rates the par-72 layout at an enormous 77.1.

Although Chicago is generally fairly flat, this is not true of the area on which Medinah is built. The holes, some of which are cleverly doglegged, rise and fall with the terrain, making club selection difficult, even without the wind. Although the greens themselves are fairly flat they are well guarded by some fiendish bunkering. Finally, water comes into play on three of the par threes, two of which measure over 183m (200yd). On the par-three 17th, the tee shot

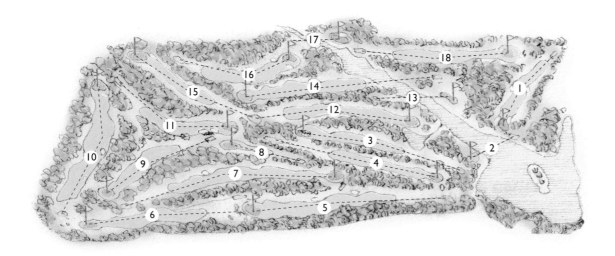

RIGHT: *At Medinah, tee shots are played across the long inlet from the expansive Lake Kadijah (named after Islamic Prophet Mohammed's wife) on no fewer than four occasions, including three par threes, the 2nd, the 13th and the 17th; and one par five, the long 14th.*

must carry all the way over Lake Kadijah (named after the wife of the Muslim prophet Mohammed).

Medinah's unusual clubhouse was built in the 1920s for an exorbitant US$600,000. With its unique architectural blend of Middle Eastern Byzantine, Louis XIV, Oriental and some Italian Renaissance elements, it includes a somewhat bizarre 18m (60ft) rotunda featuring spectacular mosaics.

Three US Open Championships have been played at Medinah – in 1949 (won by Dr Cary Middlecoff), in 1975 (won by Lou Graham) and in 1990, when 45-year-old Hale Irwin had to play 91 holes to snatch victory, becoming the oldest-ever winner of the US Open. (Those were still the days of an 18-hole playoff, which Irwin took to an extra sudden-death hole against Mike Donald.)

Another Major, the PGA Championship, was being played there in 1999 when Tiger Woods held off a spirited advance from young Spanish sensation, Sergio Garcia, to win his second Major title after his record-breaking victory in the 1997 Masters.

MEDINAH
GARY PLAYER'S VIEW

Tiger Woods won his first US PGA Championship here in 1999 and I, too, have had the pleasure of winning a Major on this very difficult course, beating Bob Charles in a playoff to win the 1988 US Senior Open.

The course has sloping greens and beautiful tall oaks that line the fairways, making it imperative to drive the ball straight. Possibly the best known of several truly demanding holes is the long par-three 17th, which requires a shot over Lake Kadijah. Talking about long, the par-five 7th stretches close to 550m (600yd), although even this does not intimidate today's long hitters.

ABOVE: *Built in the 1920s, the imposing clubhouse at Medinah has an intriguing blend of several architectural styles.*

RIGHT: *The 17th was built for the 1990 US Open. It was not a success and has been completely rebuilt.*

OAKMONT

A national landmark

OAKMONT, PENNSYLVANIA, USA

The Oakmont Country Club in Oakmont, Pennsylvania, was the brainchild of its first president Henry C Fownes, a local steel magnate who decided to build a brutally tough course that would bring even the best players to their knees. In 1904, with 150 men and 25 mule-teams, he completed the first 12 holes in just six weeks, while the remaining six were added in spring later that year.

The course, built on a stretch of flatlands in the foothills of the Alleghenies, opened with a par of 80, including a total of 220 bunkers and no fewer than eight par fives, as well as a par six. Within a year Fownes, who is said to have had a bunker fixation, added another 130, bringing the total to an unprecedented 350.

Two bunkers in particular have become legendary in world golf, namely the 'Sahara' on the 8th and the 'Church Pews' which separates the 3rd and 4th fairways. The Sahara bunker – some 73m (80yd) long and 32m (35yd) wide – reputedly took 11 truckloads of sand to fill, while the 55x37m (60x40yd) Church Pews bunker is distinguished by seven grassy ridges that run across its length.

Although bunkers may dominate the course, it is the punishing

greens that visitors remember most vividly. In the US Opens of 1927 and 1935, the winners – the Silver Scot, Tommy Armour, and Sam Parks, a local golfer who knew the course exceptionally well – scored 301 and 299, respectively. Considering that par was 288, this clearly indicates how the brutal course could make a mockery of even the best players.

Following World War II, it was agreed to make Oakmont less intimidating, so the unusually narrow fairways were widened and the number of bunkers was subsequently reduced to under 200.

Oakmont Club has long been known for doing things its own way and the US Opens of 1953 and 1962 were

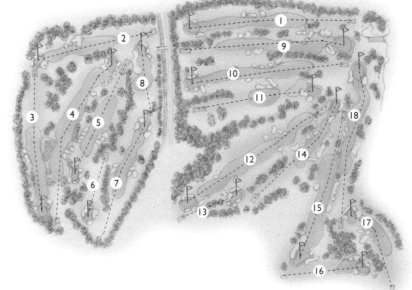

RIGHT: *Sand everywhere you look. . . the par-four 14th requires an accurate drive threaded between the numerous bunkers on each side of the fairway. Once on the putting surface, the exceptional speed of the Oakmont greens provides a further challenge.*

marred by disagreements with the US Golf Association over the rakes used to smooth the bunkers. The unique rakes left deep furrows in the sand into which trapped balls would roll – proving nearly impossible to extricate successfully. Controversy broke out again in 1983 when the players in the US Open were greeted by rough that was 23cm (9in) thick in places, meaning that anyone who missed the fairway had to hack at the ball just to get it back on to the fairway.

Given all these disagreements it is perhaps strange that Oakmont holds the record for hosting the most US Opens. All were won by star American professionals like Ben Hogan and Jack Nicklaus – until 1994, when South Africa's Ernie Els triumphed in a three-way playoff against Loren Roberts and Colin Montgomerie. Els won in a sudden-death decider after he and Roberts finished the regulation 18 with 74s, leaving the luckless Montgomerie trailing by four strokes.

Oakmont is the only course in the USA to have been declared a National Landmark, an honour bestowed in 1987.

OAKMONT

GARY PLAYER'S VIEW

Oakmont requires good course management, and you have to know it to play it well. In the old days, they used to rake the bunkers with long prongs, which left deep furrows in the sand. If you found yourself in one of those ruts, you often had to chip out sideways. Fortunately, times have changed. Today, many trees have been removed and the course is back to its original design. It is still famous for its very large, lightning-fast greens and many large bunkers — among them the notorious Church Pews.

LEFT: *The infamous Church Pews bunker lies between the 3rd and 4th holes, threatening the tee shots on both.*

PINE VALLEY

One of America's toughest

CLEMENTON, NEW JERSEY, USA

It was George Crump, owner of the Colonnades Hotel in Philadelphia, Pennsylvania, who first spotted the land on which Pine Valley now stands. An avid golfer, he used to travel from the Philadelphia Country Club to Atlantic City by train to play on a regular basis. On one such trip, he noticed the land he believed would be ideal for a golf course. He persuaded 18 of his fellow golfers each to part with US$1000 to purchase the 75ha (185 acres) of land covered with pine and oak trees, swamps and impenetrable bush.

Construction started in 1912, with Crump living in a small bungalow on site to oversee the felling of trees, laying out of fairways and construction of dams. With the assistance of Harry S Colt, the British architect who later designed Wentworth, Crump set about fulfilling his ambition of creating the most difficult course in the world.

Progress was slow. In 1918, with only 14 holes completed, Crump died, having already spent some US$250,000 of his own money to realize his dream. Fortunately, there was enough in his estate to call in Hugh Wilson, the creator

of the Merion golf course in Philadelphia, Pennsylvania, and his brother Allen, to direct construction of the remaining four holes. The result would surely have pleased Crump and it drew praise from both course designers and players of all skills levels.

Built on extremely sandy terrain, the Pine Valley course presents the ultimate challenge to golfers as they attempt to find the narrow strips of fairways dotted among vast, sandy waste areas.

With only two par fives – the 535m (585yd) 7th and the 551m (603yd) 15th – the par-70 course measures 6186m (6765yd).

Pine Valley's difficulty is legendary and there is said to be a standing bet among the members that newcomers to the course will never break 80 at their first attempt.

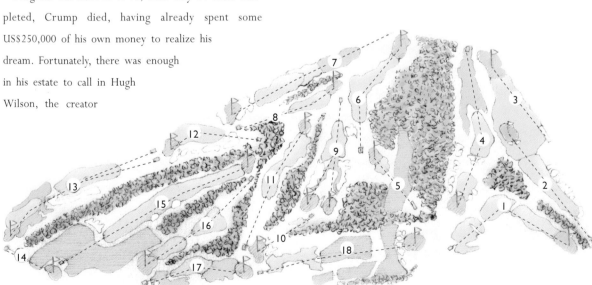

RIGHT: *The view from the tee of the 167m (184yd) par-three 14th, showing the shot that is played over water to a raised green.*

The great Arnold Palmer, about to be married and short of money, arrived to play at the course soon after triumphing in the 1954 US Amateur Championship. He took a number of bets that he would break 80 at his first attempt. Knowing he would be unable to pay if he lost, Palmer set about scoring a flawless 68 and left the course with a sizable wedding present.

Another well-documented story is of the late Woody Platt, who started with a birdie at the long par-four 1st with its typical drive over sandy wasteland. He then holed his 7-iron approach to the second for an eagle and holed-in-one at the short 3rd, which has nothing but 160m (175yd) of sand between the tee and green. At the 426m (461yd) par-four 4th, he birdied from 11m (36ft) and then returned to the

nearby clubhouse at six under par after four to contemplate the rest of his round. Apparently, he took courage from a drink or two and never made it back onto the course.

Despite its fame, Pine Valley has never hosted a Major championship, mostly because it cannot accommodate large crowds, although some believe it may be to avoid many a player's reputation being badly damaged by this tough course.

ABOVE: *The approach shot to the par-four 13th is played along a fairway entirely flanked by sandy waste areas. Pine Valley is laid out on 74ha (184 acres) of forest and marshland on the highest piece of land in the region.*

RIGHT: *At only 299m (327yd) the 8th is a short par four, downhill at that. But the problem is stopping the ball on the tiny green, many approach shots spinning back into a deep green-front bunker. The large grassy swale in the foreground awaits should the shot be struck too firmly.*

PINE VALLEY
GARY PLAYER'S VIEW

Pine Valley is pure poetry, evoking an awe-inspiring feeling much like that experienced when you set foot on Pebble Beach, St Andrews or Augusta National. A roughly cultivated, almost desert-like sandy scrub surrounds many of the greens, making the lush green fairways and putting surfaces appear to float like islands on a sea of sand and shrubs. Although people refer to it as 'the toughest, most penal golf course in the world', the architect, George Fazio, countered, 'It is only penal if you are not playing well.'

This remarkable golf club has a tiny old clubhouse whose unpretentious charm is part of Pine Valley's appeal.

THE FLORIDIAN

Florida's tranquil retreat

STUART, FLORIDA, USA

The Floridian, located alongside the Saint Lucie River near Stuart in Florida, was built in 1996 by Gary Player and was listed as one of *Golf Digest*'s 'Top 10 Best New Private Courses' that same year.

The course was constructed on what is essentially a flat piece of land, although this is hard to believe as one walks the carefully landscaped course today. Wind is a major factor on its wide-open fairways, especially in the early afternoon. The signature hole is the 5th, a 398m (435yd)

par four with a fairway that doglegs to the right and water surrounding the entire right side of the green. Measuring 6324m (6916yd) off the back tees, this par-72 layout is rated 73.5, and features almost 50 bunkers as well as flat greens that are medium to fast in speed.

This exclusive club was planned to cater for no more than 15 to 20 members. The Gary Player Design team succeeded in creating a tranquil layout for the select group that enjoys the privilege of playing it.

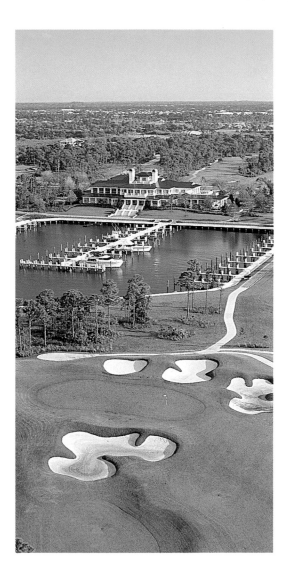

LEFT: *Florida, with its year-round temperate climate, is home to more than a thousand golf and country clubs. The Floridian, located alongside the tranquil waters of the Saint Lucie River, is one of the region's most exclusive golfing facilities.*

ABOVE RIGHT: *Clover-shaped bunkers surround the green of The Floridian's 18th green. Behind the green is the club's marina and imposing clubhouse. This exclusive club has a membership of no more than 20, one of whom is the course designer, Gary Player himself.*

THE FLORIDIAN
GARY PLAYER'S VIEW

Although The Floridian's gorgeous clubhouse is brand-new, it has the aura of one that has occupied its ground for years. It is home to some of the most interesting and coveted sporting memorabilia in the world. My design team created a course here that would be user-friendly for its small, exclusive membership. I am pleased to say that I am one of those members. I particularly love its practice facilities — the only place I know where a golfer can really practise in peace.

TPC AT JASNA POLANA

Built for viewing pleasure

PRINCETON, NEW JERSEY, USA

The concept of Tournament Players Clubs (TPCs) was started by the US PGA Tour's then commissioner Deane Beman, who wanted to provide tour players with quality golf courses that would also offer spectators the advantage of enhanced viewing areas.

Beman reasoned that development of quality facilities would alleviate the tour's dependency on the television dollar, while providing rent-free venues for tournaments. In turn, the savings in rent would generate both larger purses and greater charitable contributions by the tournaments held at TPCs.

The TPC at Sawgrass was the first to hold a US PGA Tour event, home of the prestigious Players' Championship on the tour. Since its inception 20 years ago, the TPC network continues to grow, with 30 facilities currently open or under construction. In 1999, 16 tournaments, including events on both the US PGA and US Senior Tours, were played at TPC courses.

Many top golf course architects such as Pete Dye, Tom Fazio, Arnold Palmer and Jack Nicklaus have been involved with the design of TPC facilities that encompass all forms of golf-related operations – resort facilities, corporate and private membership clubs and daily fee courses.

Started in May 1996, the TPC at Jasna Polana in Princeton is a Gary Player design. Player transformed Jasna Polana (Polish for 'Bright Meadows') from a private estate into a magnificent golfing facility suitable for all types of golfers. With its spectator mounding, it is nevertheless also an ideal venue for tournament golf.

With its serene setting and mature trees, the young course gives the impression of having been there for years. It features multiple tees, from the forward tees that give the layout a total measurement of just 4023m (4400yd), to

LEFT: *Multiple tees at the TPC at Jasna Polana cater for golfers with a variety of skill levels.* ABOVE RIGHT: *The short par-three 2nd is guarded front and back by bunkers as well as by a creek that runs in front and to the right, making the correct club selection critical.*

the tour players' tees that stretch the course to a more challenging 6492m (7100yd).

The 411m (450yd) par-four 6th hole is the most difficult of the course. Reasonably straight, it is nevertheless protected by a liberal sprinkling of bunkers on both sides of the fairway, as well as two large traps which guard the entrance to the green.

It is followed by the monstrous 549m (600yd) par-five 7th. Water is very much in evidence on the course, especially on the 16th and 17th holes, a short par four and a reasonably long par three.

TPC AT JASNA POLANA

GARY PLAYER'S VIEW

This property belonged to the late Seward Johnson of Johnson & Johnson. We were asked to design the course and use the magnificent home, filled with beautiful works of art, as the clubhouse. Today the Tournament Players Club manages the course, which hosted the Instinct Classic on the Senior Tour in 2000. Set in such luxury, the course has already been described as 'the crown jewel' of the TPC network. Laid out over this magnificent estate, with huge trees and rolling terrain, the course provides a great day of golf, not just for the pro, but for golfers of all levels.

OAKLAND HILLS

A 'monster' in Michigan

BIRMINGHAM, MICHIGAN, USA

In 1916, the dusty Maple Road in southeastern Oakland was almost a day's journey from the heartland of the US motor industry in Detroit. Undeterred by the distance, two golf enthusiasts decided to transform 400ha (988 acres) of rolling farmland lining Maple Road into a golf course. The men were Norval Hawkins, who had become Henry Ford's first accountant in 1903 and later the company's first sales manager, and Joseph Mack, who handled printing and advertising for the Ford Motor Company. On 17 June 1916, they met 46 golf-loving friends and acquaintances at the Detroit Athletic Club for the first board meeting of the Oakland Hills Country Club. The club's first members, numbering 140, each paid US$250 to join.

To design the course, the board hired famous Scottish golf course architect, Donald Ross, who had designed Royal Dornoch in Scotland and over 100 courses in the USA. Ross also later built the Scottish links-style North course on the other side of Maple Road. 'The Lord in-tended this to be a golf course!' Ross exclaimed when he first saw the landscape.

In 1917, architect C Howard Crane submitted the plan for a clubhouse modelled on George Washington's Mt Vernon home, an imposing building that still stands today. The course – a par-72 layout measuring 6450m (7108yd) from the back tees – opened the following year, when Walter Hagen was appointed as the first pro, working out of a chicken coop alongside the first hole.

Oakland Hills has hosted six US Open Championships, dating back to 1924 when Bobby Jones was upset by Cyril Walker, as well as two US PGA Championships and two US Senior Opens. Prior to the 1951 US Open, the US Golf Association called on renowned English-born course architect Robert Trent Jones Snr to modernize the Oakland Hills South course. His modified layout raised more than a few eyebrows from the field that year. The fairways were

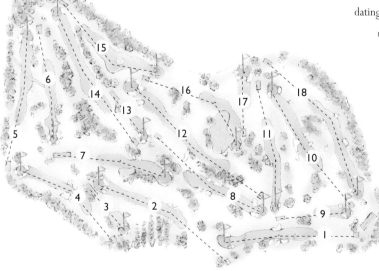

LEFT: *The 16th at Oakland Hills is a dogleg right par four played alongside a large lake. In the 1972 US PGA Championship, Gary Player played his second shot over the trees and lake onto the green, from where he made a remarkable birdie.*

narrower – some just 23m (25yd) wide – and the rough was punishing. There were also 120 bunkers strategically positioned to guard the fairway landing areas and the greens, which were also surrounded by wide, deep sand traps, many with overhanging lips. The last five holes of the course were particularly demanding and became known as the 'Fearsome Fivesome'.

American Ben Hogan came to Oakland Hills that year as the US Open defending champion. Working relentlessly at mastering the brutal layout, he steadily reduced his scores over the first three days, carding 76, 73 and 71 to go into the final round two strokes behind joint leaders Bobby Locke and Jimmy Demaret. Until then, no one had scored below 70 in the event, but Hogan proceeded to play what has come to be recognized as one of the best rounds of championship golf ever. His 67 gave him a comfortable victory over Clayton Heafner, whose 69 was the only other score to break 70. After the event, Hogan commented: 'I'm glad I brought this course, this monster, to its knees.'

The 1950s also brought other changes to Oakland Hills. Golf carts were introduced for the first time and the men's locker room was air-conditioned, although the ladies' locker room in the basement remained hot and muggy in the summer. It was not until 1975 that a bridge over Maple Road was built to connect the two courses and the ladies moved out of the basement into their own dressing room above ground.

Although at times in its history Oakland Hills had to advertise for members, today it has a waiting list of two-and-a-half years and the initiation fee is a princely US$48,000. Firmly entrenched on the championship roster, it is scheduled to host the US Amateur in 2002, its first Ryder Cup in 2003, and its third US PGA Championship in 2008.

Detroit has expanded considerably since the early days of the 20th century when Oakland Hills was established by Hawkins, Mack and their friends. Today, the course lies in the suburbs on the outskirts of the city. Although not a scenic layout in the mould of Augusta or Pebble Beach, it is a formidable golf course that forms a worthy challenge for the world's best golfers in the new millennium.

OAKLAND HILLS
GARY PLAYER'S VIEW

Oakland Hills is a demanding yet fair test of golf. Only the best putters can handle these fast and severely contoured greens.

During the 1972 PGA Championship, the 16th was the hole that determined the outcome of the tournament. I had to hit my approach shot from 137m (150yd) out, with a tall willow tree blocking my view of the flagstick on the green, just beyond the water hazard. Although I could not see the flag, a spectator had left a seat stick right in line with the hole so I aimed at that, hitting the ball through the top of the tree. It stopped just three feet away from the cup, leaving an easy putt. The birdie gave me a two-stroke lead and the victory. Today, a brass plaque at the 16th hole commemorates this shot.

RIGHT: *The slightly elevated green of the par-four 6th hole at Oakland Hills is surrounded by bunkers and tall trees. Laid out in 1917, the course is situated on a piece of land that architect Donald Ross claimed 'the Lord had intended to be a golf course'.*

WINGED FOOT

A 'man-sized' golf course

WEST COURSE, MAMARONECK, NEW YORK, USA

In the early 1920s, AW Tillinghast was instructed by members of the New York Athletic Club to construct two 'man-sized' 18-hole golf courses at Mamaroneck, New York. Tillinghast, one of America's great golf course architects and the designer of the renowned Baltusrol Golf Club in nearby New Jersey, cleared 7800 trees and moved 7200 tonnes of rock, eventually creating the Winged Foot East and West courses that opened for play in 1923.

While the East course is considered to be more attractive, the West course is regarded as a true championship test, playing 229m (250yd) longer, at 6360m (6956yd) off the back tees. It has hosted the US PGA Championship once and the US Open four times. For America's national championship, the par-72 layout (rated 73.5) is made considerably tougher by converting the par-five 9th and 16th into par fours to play to a total par of 70. Ten of the course's

12 par fours measure over 366m (400yd) and, although the layout undoubtedly favours the longer hitter, its 60 bunkers – including at least two deep bunkers near every green – also put a premium on accuracy. All the greens, raised and subtly contoured, are constructed in Tillinghast's trademark pear shape.

In 1929, professional golfers from around the country came to Winged Foot to examine Tillinghast's creation and participate in the first US Open hosted there. The great Bobby Jones, already the winner of two US Opens and undoubtedly the favourite, pleased the crowds by tearing up the course on day one with a superb 69. However, his 75 the following day provided a dose of Winged Foot reality and, at the end of 72 holes of regulation play, Jones was tied for the lead with Al Espinosa on 294, requiring them to return for the customary 36-hole playoff. Jones, who had

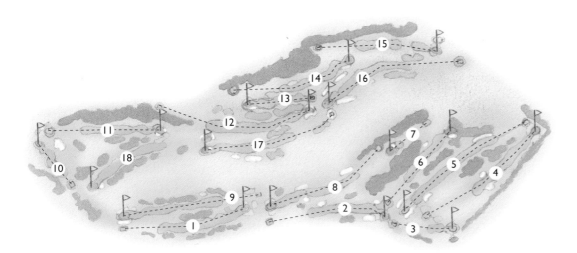

RIGHT: *American Davis Love III sinks the winning putt on the 18th green at Winged Foot to take the 1997 US PGA Championship and lift the coveted Wanamaker Trophy. The victory marked Love's first-ever win in a Major championship.*

previously lost two US Opens in playoffs, did not falter on this occasion, opening with a solid 72 while Espinosa, unaccustomed to the pressure, shot an embarrassing 84. Jones closed with another brilliant 69 to win the playoff by a staggering 23 strokes and take his third US Open title.

The US Open returned to Winged Foot in 1959 when Billy Casper was the winner, while Hale Irwin was victorious in 1974 with a seven-over-par total of 287, and Fuzzy Zoeller defeated Greg Norman in a playoff in 1984.

Then, in 1997 when Winged Foot was chosen to host the year's final Major, the US PGA Championship, immensely talented golfer, Davis Love III, finally put to rest the 'best player never to have won a Major' tag with a convincing victory over Justin Leonard.

While Winged Foot Golf Club's affiliation with the New York Athletic Club has long since ended, the club has always retained the winged foot logo – and this challenging layout remains a 'man-sized' test, even for today's big-hitters.

WINGED FOOT

GARY PLAYER'S VIEW

Among the toughest and best courses I have played, Winged Foot is long, with elevated greens and excellent bunkers. Designer AW Tillinghast obviously thought like a golfer, commenting about this course: 'The contouring of the greens places a great premium on the placement of the drives...' Winged Foot's East course virtually matches the West course for design excellence and quality. Golf fans will get a good look at Tillinghast's talent during the 2002 US Open, played on Long Island at Bethpage State Park's Black Course, the first US Open venue ever at a true 'public' (rather than a high-end daily-fee) golf course.

LEFT: *The green of Winged Foot's par-five 12th hole is elevated and pear-shaped, a feature that is a trademark of renowned course designer AW Tillinghast, who built the course in 1923.*

ABOVE: *Gary Player, pictured playing at Winged Foot during the 1974 US Open, earned the nickname 'the Black Knight' as a result of his golfing attire.*

PINEHURST

America's golfing mecca

NO. 2 COURSE, PINEHURST, NORTH CAROLINA, USA

The Pinehurst story began late in the 19th century when Boston manufacturer, James Tufts, purchased 2023ha (5000 acres) of land in the Sandhills region of North Carolina with a view to developing a hotel and leisure resort that would offer wealthy East Coast residents an escape from bitter northern winters. Soon recognizing the need for golfing facilities, Tufts had an 18-hole layout built by an amateur course designer. Later named Pinehurst No. 1, this course was opened in 1898.

The Tufts family had previously met a young Scottish professional-greenkeeper, Donald Ross, at Dornoch. In 1898 Ross emigrated to work at Oakley Country Club in Massachusetts, where, once again he caught the eye of the Tufts. He was soon invited to become winter golf professional at the new resort. After redesigning Pinehurst

No. 1, he began work on what was to become a masterpiece of golf course architecture, Pinehurst No. 2. Although he went on to build, design or redesign over 400 golf courses throughout North America – including two other courses at Pinehurst and several more in the region – Pinehurst No. 2 is regarded by many as Ross's best work.

Drawing on his Scottish heritage, Ross introduced mounding, extensive bunkering and raised, contoured greens to the barren piece of land to create a layout that is demanding yet fair. Although generally large, the greens are convex, causing any inaccurate or misdirected shot to roll off into the surrounding collection areas. Once the golfer is on the green, the subtle slopes demand a deft touch with the putter.

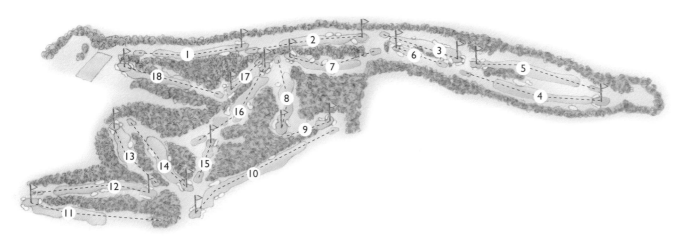

RIGHT: *The 17th hole at Pinehurst No. 2 is a par-three of 174m (190yd) played through a grove of tall pines. Typical of the putting surfaces at Pinehurst, the green is slightly raised, directing wayward balls into the large bunkers on either side.*

For the 1999 US Open the course measured 6561m (7175yd), playing to a tough par of 70, and, with Donald Ross's raised greens protected by collars of thick rough, scoring was high. Normally the fairway landing areas are generous, and the bunkers – numbering 109 in all – and greens are generally visible from the tees. Although the exhausted timberland on which Ross laid out the course was relatively open at the time, the pines that gave the area its name have grown thick and tall. Today, they line each fairway, creating a wonderful atmosphere of solitude and tranquillity.

Pinehurst's relative inaccessibility has meant that its No. 2 course has hosted fewer championship golf events than befits a layout of its stature. In 1936, it hosted its first Major, the US PGA Championship, but it was 63 years before the course returned to the Major roster when Payne Stewart held off Phil Mickelson to win his second US Open title in 1999. America's national championship is scheduled to return to Pinehurst No. 2 in 2005.

The course also hosted the 1951 Ryder Cup, the 1991 Tour Championship and the 1994 US Senior Open.

Pinehurst has always maintained strong links with the amateur game, and the 1962 US Amateur Championship was staged here. Pinehurst No. 1 hosted the annual North and South Amateur Championship from 1901 to 1908, after which it moved to Pinehurst No. 2, which has been its home ever since. Richard S Tufts, the grandson of Pinehurst's founding father, made a major contribution to the development of the game in the USA, and was also one of the founders of the World Amateur Team Championship. Now known as the Eisenhower Trophy, it is regarded as the world's most prestigious amateur team golf tournament.

Pinehurst No. 2 may have hosted few great events, but it has produced several great champions. Ben Hogan won his first professional title here in 1940, Jack Nicklaus won the North and South in 1959, and Walter Hagen won the event on three occasions. The incomparable Babe Zaharias triumphed in the North and South Women's Amateur in 1947.

Other worthy Pinehurst champions whose photographs line the corridors of the stately clubhouse are Jack Nicklaus's son, Jack Nicklaus II, Curtis Strange, Corey Pavin, Billy Andrade and Davis Love III.

Today, the Pinehurst Resort and Country Club is America's premier golf resort. It offers golfing pilgrims a choice of eight 18-hole championship golf courses open for play all year round (the construction of a ninth golf course got underway in the autumn of 2000). Futhermore, within a radius of 25km (16 miles) of the Pinehurst resort are another two dozen golf courses bearing signs of the influence of a host of great golf course architects, making the area a golfing mecca. They include Robert Trent Jones, Tom and George Fazio, Ellis Maples and Rees Jones.

Many of the world's rich and famous have holidayed at Pinehurst over the past 100 or so years, including Bing Crosby, Michael Jordan, Oprah Winfrey, the Rockefellers and the DuPonts, while Amelia Earhart actually landed her plane at the resort's airstrip.

PINEHURST
GARY PLAYER'S VIEW

Pinehurst's No. 2 course is a classic in every way. Few courses challenge me mentally as much as this one, testing every aspect of my game. It is also one of the world's most enjoyable courses despite being extremely demanding. The greens, with their convex bowl-like shapes, demand precise iron approach shots or the ball will roll down and off the greens into adjacent chipping areas. Set among the stately Carolina pines, the course has a natural beauty all its own.

RIGHT: *Pinehurst No. 2 hosted the 1994 US Senior Open. This view of the par-five 16th shows the course's only water feature, which requires a carry of 165m (180yd) off the tee.*

CONGRESSIONAL

A true test of endurance

BLUE COURSE, BETHESDA, MARYLAND, USA

Ten kilometres north of Washington DC, in the rolling green hills of northern Maryland, lies Congressional Country Club with its lush parkland layout, tall trees and large expanses of water overlooked by a stately white clubhouse. Originally designed in 1922 by amateur golfer Devereaux Emmett after two congressmen decided to establish a country club on the 139ha (343 acres) of land, the course was officially opened by US President Calvin Coolidge in 1924. Secretary of Commerce Herbert Hoover was inaugurated as the club's first president, with luminaries such as Woodrow Wilson as founding life members.

The original golf course, which later became known as Congressional's 'Blue' course, served members of the private club well until 1957 when, with a view to attracting championship events to the course, Robert Trent Jones Snr laid out nine new holes of what was to become the 'Gold' course.

His efforts were rewarded two years later when the US Golf Association (USGA) staged the Women's Amateur Championship there. Trent Jones also updated one of Emmett's original nines, making changes such as replacing the par-three finishing hole with a long par four. These improvements secured the US Open Championship for Congressional in 1964.

The 1964 US Open will long be remembered for the heroic performance of eventual winner, Ken Venturi. The lay-out that year measured over 6400m (7000yd), the longest course in US Open history, and two of the par fives had been converted to par fours. Back then, the last round of the US Open was played over 36 holes on the Saturday, the USGA believing 'endurance as well as skill shall be a requisite of a national champion'. On that Saturday morning in 1964, the golfers' endurance was severely tested in sweltering sunshine and high humidity.

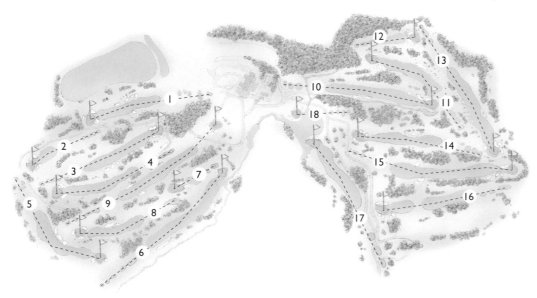

RIGHT: *Congressional's par-three 7th features a narrow, tree-lined approach to a lightning-fast, sloping and undulating green.*

Ken Venturi, not a physically strong man, finished the morning round in 66, although he faltered towards the end and was near collapse from heat stroke on the 18th hole. After rest and rehydration during the break, he was accompanied by a doctor and a thermos of iced tea as he set out for the second round – during which he carded an unforgettable 70 to claim the US Open title by four strokes.

In 1990, Rees Jones, the son of Robert Trent Jones, was called in to modify the course further, a father-son combination that resulted in the creation of a superb championship layout.

Since 1964, Congressional has four times hosted the Kemper Open on the US PGA Tour, and been the venue for three other Majors. Dave Stockton won his second PGA Championship here in 1976, while in 1995 Tom Weiskopf edged out Jack Nicklaus to win the US Senior Open. In 1997, 27-year-old South African Ernie Els emerged on the Sunday from a four-man pack on the back nine to capture his second US Open title in four years. Els shot a one-under-par 69 to finish one stroke ahead of Scotland's Colin Montgomerie, and two ahead of second and third round leader, Tom Lehman. This was the first time the US Open had been played on the full 'Blue'

course, as played by Congressional's members, with the championship ending on a 174m (190yd) par three – unusual for a Major championship. (In previous events, two holes had been borrowed from Congressional's 'Gold' course to create a more conventional finish.)

During the US Open, the 6th and 10th holes, both par fives, are converted to par fours, making it a par-70 course that favours the long hitter. Congressional's rolling hills and summer heat, the length of its layout (7059m/7530yd from the championship tees), plus the severe rough and lightning-fast greens can make this excellent course a gruelling challenge.

CONGRESSIONAL
GARY PLAYER'S VIEW

Congressional's world-class 'Blue' golf course is long and tough, with undulating greens. You have to hit the ball straight off of the tee, and you need a lot of patience. It is one of the few championship courses that finishes with a par three. However, there is no rule saying a course cannot finish with a par three – East Lake in Atlanta and Alister Mackenzie's gem, Pasatiempo in Santa Cruz, California, being two other examples that do.

FAR LEFT: *Congressional's par-five 10th is played as a par four during the US Open. The course hosted the event most recently in 1997 when South Africa's Ernie Els beat Scotland's Colin Montgomerie by one stroke to claim his second Major title. A stream runs down the length of the right-hand side of the 10th fairway, feeding a pond alongside the deep, pear-shaped green.*

LEFT: *Congressional is a long and demanding course. The 507m (554yd) par-five 15th hole requires two long and accurate shots for big hitters going for the green in two seeking a two-putt birdie.*

WENTWORTH (WEST)

Through fir and silver birch

WEST COURSE, VIRGINIA WATER, SURREY, ENGLAND

Wentworth in Surrey is widely regarded as one of the best inland courses in England. Construction began in 1923, on one of the first facilities in England based on the US country club idea, in which golf was not the only leisure activity available. It was also one of the earliest English developments in which houses were built alongside the fairways.

Two 18-hole courses and a short, nine-hole course were designed by renowned golf course architect Harry Colt. The shorter East course was completed first, followed by the West course in 1927. The West became the championship course and because of its length – it is now over 6400m (7000yd) – was nicknamed 'The Burma Road'. A third 18-hole course, called the Edinburgh, was added later, designed collaboratively by John Jacobs, Bernard Gallacher and Gary Player.

The West course, set among woodlands of firs and Silver Birch, is designed in the traditional style of parkland courses, without the space for spectators that modern tournament courses demand today. Nevertheless, Wentworth remains the venue for two of the world's most prestigious tournaments: the World Matchplay and the Volvo PGA Championship.

The World Matchplay was started by Mark McCormack's International Management Group (IMG) in 1964 as a show-

case for the 'Big Three', as they were then known: Jack Nicklaus, Arnold Palmer and Gary Player. High-profile matchplay tournaments had been rare since 1957 when the US PGA Championship 'converted' from a matchplay event to a purely strokeplay tournament. The invitation-only World Matchplay continues to be regarded as the most important matchplay event in world professional golf and boasts many fine champions. Gary Player has won the title no fewer than five times, while other multiple champions include Greg Norman, Ernie Els and the most-feared matchplay opponent of them all, Spain's Seve Ballesteros.

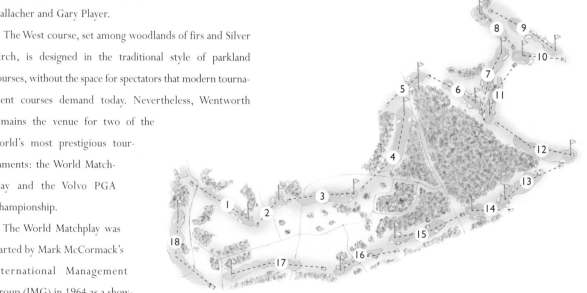

RIGHT: *An aerial view of the West course at Wentworth showing the par-four 11th hole on the left and the par-four 7th on the right.*

108

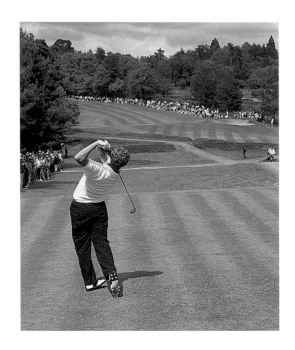

The PGA European Tour has its headquarters at Wentworth, so it is no surprise that one of its most prestigious tournaments, the Volvo PGA Championship, is held here each May. All the big names take part and winners at Wentworth have included Bernhard Langer, Nick Faldo, Ian Woosnam, and Colin Montgomerie. The World Matchplay is squeezed into the schedule in October, just as southern England's weather turns bitterly cold once more.

With their extended television coverage, the closing holes at Wentworth have become extremely well known. The 17th is a long (522m/571yd) doglegging par five whose fairway slopes to the right while the hole curves through trees in the opposite direction. This makes a perfectly placed drive vital if the green is to be reached in two. The 18th, oddly enough also a par five, is substantially shorter at only some 457m (500yd), but its green is well guarded by large bunkers on either side.

Ending with two par fives has made for many exciting finishes in both matchplay and strokeplay events there, with players often 'going for broke' on those holes.

As it is not a links course, Wentworth will never be included on the roster of Open Championship courses, but it has hosted a match between the professionals of the USA versus those of Great Britain and Ireland (a forerunner to the Ryder Cup). In 1956, it also hosted the Canada Cup (now the World Cup).

WENTWORTH

GARY PLAYER'S VIEW

I am a member at Wentworth, where I have won five World Matchplay Championships, a record I proudly share with Seve Ballesteros. Although I first played Wentworth West in 1955, it seems like only yesterday! The holes on the back nine are very familiar due to the exposure they receive each year during the World Matchplay telecasts. Wentworth West closes with back-to-back par fives – a bit unusual for a championship course, but it succeeds magnificently here. This course really has a very special place in my heart and is a great test of golf.

ABOVE: *Colin Montgomerie of Scotland, teeing off at Wentworth, where he has won the Volvo PGA Championship on three consecutive occasions from 1998 to 2000.*

RIGHT: *The scene at the green of the par-five 18th during tournament time. The West course is home to the annual PGA Championship as well as the World Matchplay.*

FIVE NATIONS

A truly international club

The Five Nations Country Club was created when a leading US property development company, Acquest International, sought to develop a truly international country club in western Europe. A suitable location within easy driving time of Belgium, Luxembourg, the Netherlands, France and Germany was targeted and, in 1988, a perfect property was found in the grounds of an existing golf course close to the Ardennes in Belgium. Here, Gary Player set about redesigning the course and clubhouse to international tournament standards.

The club is situated in the centre of the Brussels–Luxembourg–Bonn triangle, with these cities and their related international airports all within an hour's drive. Set on 115ha (284 acres) of rolling, forested hills, the course features a number of holes that run along natural valleys, some of them bordered on the one side by a river and lined with woods on the other. This type of layout demands a golfer's utmost concentration and is a trademark of Gary Player's designs.

Although it is challenging, the course has multiple tee positions to enable golfers of all levels to excel. A significant elevation difference between the highest and lowest points on the course results in a number of holes playing dramatically downhill and provides for both exciting golf and magnificent panoramic views of the surrounding picturesque villages and chateaux. With its vantage points, the course is well suited for large spectator galleries, making it an ideal tournament venue.

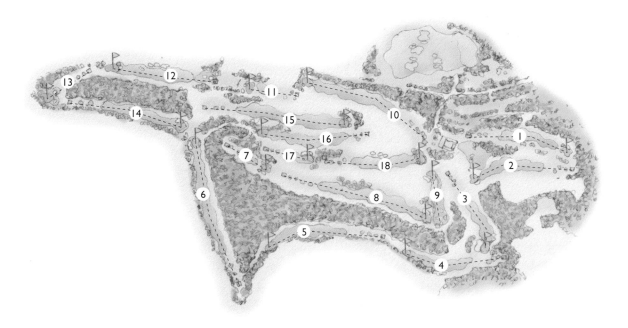

RIGHT: *The course at Five Nations was carved out of indigenous forest areas, utilizing existing streams as water features and hazards within the playing corridors.*

The imposing clubhouse with its stone walls and cobbled courtyard is typical of the Belgian architectural heritage of the region. It has been carefully modernized to provide all the expected conveniences of a leading international golf club.

ABOVE: *Five Nations Country Club is so named because of its proximity to four different European nations – Luxembourg, the Netherlands, France and Germany – from its location just south of Liège in Belgium.*

FIVE NATIONS
GARY PLAYER'S VIEW

The course is located just south of Liège, the cultural centre of French-speaking Belgium and an important transportation hub and industrial city that was largely rebuilt after damage during World War II. The property has magnificent natural features so our design team had to do very little to create a wonderfully peaceful and beautiful golf course. Often the finest golf courses around the world are those where the entire layout clearly presented itself to the designer when he first looked at the land – actually, I would have to say that the architect at Five Nations Country Club was God.

CHANTILLY

French country charm

PARIS, FRANCE

Situated just 40km (25 miles) north of Paris, Chantilly is widely regarded as the finest course in France. Dating back to 1908, it has hosted the French Open Championship on more than 10 occasions, as well as other important events on the European golfing calendar. In 1913, Englishman George Duncan won the first French Open here with a total of 304 – still the highest winning total in the event's history.

After a break of some 14 years the French Open returned to Chantilly in 1988 when England's Nick Faldo triumphed with a four-round total of 274. The following year Faldo defended his title, again at Chantilly, bettering his four-round total by one shot.

Despite its woodland setting, the course itself is fairly open. However, punishing rough makes this 6597m (7214yd) course among the toughest in Europe. In the early 1920s, Tom Simpson, who had redesigned parts of the Old Course at Ballybunion, was commissioned to redesign some of the holes that make up today's championship course. Ironically, considering the furore over the bunker that he added to Ballybunion, one of Simpson's major changes was to remove a number of bunkers. Although much

of his work was badly damaged during World War II, the character imprinted by his changes is still in evidence today.

The course has three par fives and four uncompromising par threes, three of them more than 183m (200yd) long. Eight of the par fours are over 384m (420yd) long and have narrow fairways to add to the challenge facing the golfer. The 13th is particularly memorable, needing a solid long

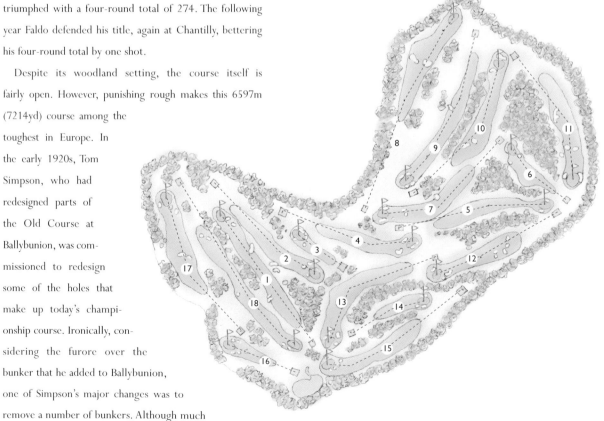

RIGHT: *The par-three 14th is played from elevated tees through Chantilly's typically dense forest, making club selection tricky.*

drive down the middle of the fairway to open up the approach to the green on this sharp dogleg left, before requiring a tough second shot over a deep grassy hollow to a green surrounded by trees. Par on this hole is certainly a good score, especially in the midst of the pressure associated with tournament play.

The final three holes form a loop, taking play out and back from the clubhouse, the 16th another of those long par threes, and the 17th a solid, curving par four plentifully bunkered in the driving zone. The 18th, at nearly 550m (600yd), is an uncompromising par five that requires three well-struck shots to find the green and complete the round.

Chantilly is perhaps better known for its famous racecourse and equestrian centre, as well as the opulent Château de Chantilly and its art treasures.

CHANTILLY
GARY PLAYER'S VIEW

Chantilly embraces the tradition of golf in a country not usually associated with the game. It is also associated with horses which, along with golf, are the passion of my life. The quaint little town with its historic castle surrounded by a lake has all the charm of the French countryside, and the region is well-known for its lace and cream. The golf course itself has a wonderful atmosphere, while the clubhouse boasts a magnificent fireplace and superb food. This is golf graced with a truly French joie-de-vivre.

RIGHT TOP: *The final three holes start in front of the magnificent clubhouse at Chantilly. The 16th and 17th are played away to the end of the course.*

RIGHT: *The long par-four 11th features a two-tier green, making the approach shot critical if the player is to have a chance at birdie.*

SPORTING CLUB BERLIN

Shades of Scotland outside Berlin

NICK FALDO COURSE, BERLIN, GERMANY

Three of golf's true masters, from three different nations, have each created an 18-hole championship golf course at the Kempinski Hotel Sporting Club near Berlin in Germany. The three are England's Nick Faldo, winner of six Majors, the USA's Arnold Palmer, winner of six Major titles and three Seniors Major titles, and Germany's own Bernhard Langer, twice a Masters champion.

Of the three layouts, it is the Nick Faldo course that is regarded as the best golf course in Germany. Opened in 1996, it measures all of 6445m (7048yd) off the back tees and plays to a par of 72 although it is rated 74. It has already earned a place on the European championship roster, hosting the German Open in 1999 and the World Amateur Team Championship in 2000. Into his demanding layout, Faldo has incorporated elements of a Scottish links course in the form of deep pot bunkers, rolling fairways and high rough, all of which place a premium on placement. The course has grown rapidly in stature in Europe, with a leading golf publication ranking it among Europe's 10 best.

Opened in 1995, the exclusive Sporting Club Berlin on the picturesque lake, Scharmutzelsee, also offers tennis, horse riding and sailing to its members.

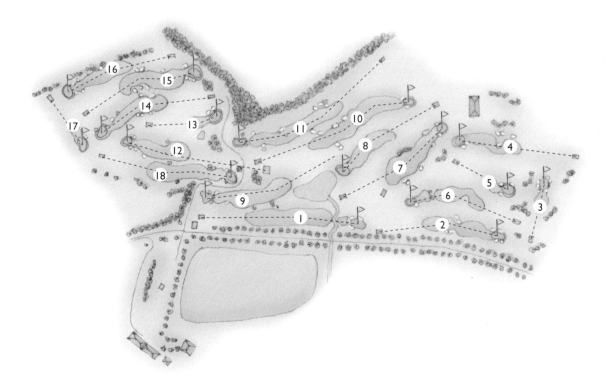

ABOVE RIGHT: *A view of the 9th green of the Nick Faldo course at Sporting Club Berlin. The course hosted the 1999 German Open, won by Sweden's Jarmo Sandelin.*

SPORTING CLUB BERLIN

GARY PLAYER'S VIEW

The success of German star, Bernard Langer, together with the opening of a world-class course near Berlin capable of hosting the German Open, has greatly increased golf's popularity in Germany. The Nick Faldo course has received high marks from European PGA Tour professionals. Of course, the fact that Germany's favourite golfing son has also designed a course here has done much to increase the profile of the game.

CLUB ZUR VAHR

The toughest 18 in Europe

GARLSTEDT, GERMANY

The Garlstedter Heide course at Bremen's sports and leisure facility, Club zur Vahr, is rated as one of Europe's top championship layouts. Constructed over 85ha (210 acres) of undulating terrain covered with heavy forest and heath, the course's narrow fairways are lined with thick groves of tall trees. Many of the holes are doglegs, and the course demands long and accurate driving to open up the green for the second shot. Miss-hit shots find the thick undergrowth among the pines and Silver Birches and are heavily punished. The course has so many natural hazards that the designer had to create very few additional ones and there are fewer than 30 bunkers, with all but one positioned near the greens.

Although golf has been played over the nine-hole Bremen course nearby since the turn of the century, the 18-hole championship layout was only constructed in 1970, when former German Junior Champion August Weyhausen brought in the former German Amateur Champion turned golf course architect, Bernhard von Limburger, to create the course.

Von Limburger built a layout that was enjoyable for the social golfer using the facilities of the sports and leisure complex but, when stretched to its maximum length of 6535m (7147yd), the course offered a formidable test for the world's best golfers. Playing to a par of 74 and rated 75, the course poses a challenge to the golfer's intelligence. On many occasions, decisive strategic thinking is required to choose between paths, while trees provide a constant threat.

A year after it opened, Club zur Vahr's Garstedter Heide course hosted the German Open Championship, won by England's Neil Coles with a 17-under-par total of 279. Coles, along with Australia's Peter Thomson, set the course record of 68 during the event. The course hosted the German Open on two subsequent occasions, in 1975 and, most recently, in 1985, when it was won by Germany's own Bernhard Langer. The event was shortened to 54 holes of regulation play due to rain delays, with Langer beating Zimbabwe's Mark McNulty and England's Michael McLean by seven strokes to collect his third German Open title.

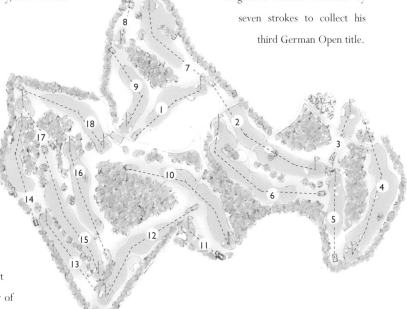

CLUB ZUR VAHR
GARY PLAYER'S VIEW

Architect Bernhard von Limburger's strategic gem has for years enjoyed a reputation as one of Europe's best golf courses. The layout is carved through massive conifer .trees, demanding strategic thinking and a range of shots. Until the latter part of the 1960s, Germany — like many other European countries — did not concern itself with building what might be called internationally recognized championship golf courses. Club zur Vahr stands as a clear example of 'early' world-class golf course architecture in mainland Europe. Now, as the courses at Sporting Club Berlin show, Europe enjoys its own Golden Age of superb golf course architectural design.

LEFT: *The green of Club zur Vahr's long par-five 2nd hole can only be reached in two after a drive down the left side of the fairway which must avoid the trees and dense undergrowth. A stream crosses the fairway 282m (300yd) from the tee, with a pond a little further on, while two trees positioned in the centre of the fairway add to the complexity of the hole.*

ABOVE: *The fairways at Club zur Vahr are lined with tall trees and dense undergrowth, compounding the demands of this long and difficult golf course.*

EL SALER

Golf on the Mediterranean

El Saler Golf Club, near Valencia on the east coast of Spain, presents an intriguing mix of links-style holes and parkland elements. This 18-hole championship golf course, measuring 6485m (7092yd) off the back tees, covers an unusual combination of terrain, from tall umbrella pines that line the fairways and surround the greens on the inland parts of the course, to spectacular coastal holes among the sand dunes beside the Gulf of Valencia, where cool sea breezes off the Mediterranean temper the summer heat. This all makes for a truly fascinating and varied golfing experience.

The contrast of styles at El Saler is best illustrated by the first hole, a typically parkland par four measuring 400m (437yd) and doglegging right through tall pines, and the 17th, a demanding par three of 195m (213yd) that is played to a green surrounded by bunkers and set in Scottish-style linksland. There are few more demanding closing holes than that at El Saler, played from a

tee high in the dunes to a fairway that is narrowed by savage rough and bunkers before curving left to a closely guarded green.

El Saler was designed by Spanish golfer and course architect Javier Arana, who also designed the well-known courses of Club de Campo in Madrid and El Prat in Barcelona. El Saler is undoubtedly Arana's masterpiece, but it wasn't until the spread of championship golf in Europe during the 1970s that it became fully appreciated.

El Saler is an established venue on the European Tour: it hosted the Spanish Open in 1984 and 1989, the Turespaña Open Mediterrania in 1993, and the Turespaña Masters in 1999. El Saler's most memorable championship event was the 1984 Spanish Open when German golfer Bernhard Langer came back from seven strokes behind to win with an amazing course-record 62 on the final day, shooting nine birdies in 11 holes from the 5th.

LEFT: *El Saler's coastal holes are built among dunes, covered in Mesembryanthemums, on Scottish links-style terrain on the Mediterranean.*

Langer was then at the peak of his playing career and he went on to win the Masters at Augusta National in 1985. He rated this period as his best golfing years, and El Saler as one of Europe's best layouts. Langer returned to El Saler in 1989 to win his second Spanish Open title.

ABOVE: *El Saler's demanding 195m (213yd) par-three 17th hole is set on links-like terrain close to the shore. The green is surrounded by large bunkers and scrub, requiring a long and accurate tee shot.*

EL SALER
GARY PLAYER'S VIEW

This is a wonderful course set on the seaside a short distance south of Valencia. It has a links character, yet heads inland into heavily wooded country as well. From the back tees, it is a true championship test for any player. I especially like four holes: the par-five 5th that heads towards dunes along the Mediterranean, finishing on a bi-level green divided lengthwise; the short, tight par-four 8th with its true links feel; the charming par-three 9th; and the fantastic 18th, which is a very challenging par four. This world-class course should not be missed by any golfer who may be travelling in Spain.

VALDERRAMA

A Trent Jones classic

SOTOGRANDE, SPAIN

Valderrama is set among the rolling hills of the Sotogrande area of Spain's Costa del Sol. The course, originally called Los Aves, was laid out in 1975 by Robert Trent Jones Snr, who always considered it one of his finest creations.

Described as typically American, the course boasts many features supporting this characterization: vast teeing areas, massive greens with severe slopes, enormous bunkers and plenty of water.

Set among hundreds of cork trees on what was originally a Cork Oak plantation, the course does not demand great length off the tees, but a premium is placed on accuracy – both from the tee and in terms of 'placing' the ball on the correct section of the green with the approach shot.

In 1985 it was bought by a consortium headed by Spanish industrialist Jaime Ortiz-Patino, and Trent Jones was once again called in to revamp the layout. He tightened the driving line on several holes, placing greater emphasis on approach shots and generally toughening it up.

For some years Valderrama was the scene of the climax of the PGA European Tour's season, the late-season Volvo Masters. But in 1997 it acquired a greater international significance when it hosted the Ryder Cup, the first course in continental Europe to do so. Here Spanish golfing hero, Severiano Ballesteros, captained the European team to a single-point victory over an American team, which included the young Tiger Woods for the first time.

Ironically, it was Ballesteros who remodelled the 17th hole at Valderrama, easily the most controversial hole on the course. A par five, which at 467m (511yd) is easily reachable in two, it has two large humps in the middle of the fairway that can block off the approach to the green. As a well-struck, well-directed drive can be severely

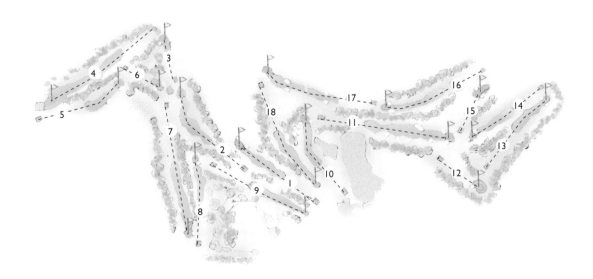

RIGHT: *The green of the 500m (547yd) par-five 4th is protected by water all the way around the right half as the golfer approaches it.*

punished, it is felt that luck plays too great a part in a player's success on this penultimate hole.

In addition to the humps, the driving area is protected by fairway bunkers and the fairways incline sharply towards the distant water, making long-iron shots to the green extremely difficult. Layed-up shots can often trickle into the water short of the green as the slope takes the ball towards the water.

Once over the water, the green also slopes severely towards the water in front which means any ball with too much backspin can also find a watery grave. But then who said golf was meant to be fair?

In 1999 Valderrama became home to one of the US$5 million World Golf Championship tournaments that carry a first prize of US$1 million.

As the jewel in the golfers' paradise that is the Costa del Sol, Valderrama has become the model for other developments that continue to mushroom along Spain's idyllic south coast.

VALDERRAMA
GARY PLAYER'S VIEW

This golf course, one of the best in Europe and the world, is dotted with hundreds of cork trees and offers wonderful views of the Mediterranean Sea. Valderrama's owner and president, Jaime Ortiz-Patino, built this course to strict environmental standards from the start, and I applaud that. It is the toughest course on the European Tour, prompting Nick Faldo to say in 1992: 'You have to play like God out there to shoot par.' Well, you know what they say: par is a good score.

RIGHT: *The approach to the green of the controversial par-five 17th showing the severe run-off into the water hazard from both the fairway and the green. The controversy centres on the contention that the large humps that block the approach to the green mean that luck plays too great a role in success or failure here.*

MANNA

A Japanese garden

CHIBA, JAPAN

The Gary Player-designed golf course at Manna Country Club near Chiba, east of Tokyo in Japan, is a parkland-style layout with the feel of a Japanese garden. Opened in October 1996, it is constructed on gently undulating land with tall, indigenous trees lining each hole. Its perfectly manicured fairways and tees, with greens of *Zoysia Japonica* and Bent grass, form a dramatic contrast with the white bunker sand and steep, brownish bunker faces, constructed from indigenous clay.

There are a number of streams on this 18-hole, championship-length layout measuring 6605m (7223yd) from the back tees. The signature hole is the scenic par-four 9th, which is 398m (435yd) long and has a stream running along the left side of the playing area.

The unusual clubhouse, designed in the style of an old European castle, was built of rock imported from the USA, while the luxurious interior was designed and finished by Italian craftsmen. The clubhouse also features a Gary Player Golf Academy and practice area, with a Japanese instructor certified to teach the Gary Player Method.

Japan has experienced burgeoning interest in the game of golf in recent years, and Gary Player has created no fewer than thirteen 18-hole golf courses in this country where land is at such a high premium. Manna Country Club has even con-

structed a second course with ageing Japanese citizens in mind. Among its attractions are eight health-check stations equipped with machines allowing golfers to measure heart rate and blood pressure, telephones in each booth so they can call a doctor in an emergency, and a monorail — complete with side platform for golf carts — to transport them from the clubhouse to the starting point.

RIGHT AND FAR RIGHT: *The undulating terrain, scenic elevation changes, tall trees and an unusual bunkering style are typical of the Manna Country Club layout. Note the steep, brown clay bunker faces which contrast with the white bunker sand.*

MANNA

GARY PLAYER'S VIEW

My favourite golf course in Japan, Manna is where we designed a dramatic style of bunkering for the first time in this country. The traps have hard faces so the ball never becomes buried in them. The bunkers have a formal appearance similar to elements found in a Japanese garden, though on a grander scale. The bunkers are yellowish-brown in colour, turning a darker, more dramatic colour when it rains. Manna Country Club is probably one of the five best-bunkered golf courses in the world. The course also has some dramatic elevation changes, while its beautiful trees create the feel of a paradise here.

ERINVALE

Golf in the winelands

SOMERSET WEST, SOUTH AFRICA

Erinvale in Somerset West, some 50km (30 miles) outside Cape Town, was one of South Africa's first estate courses to be designed with homes built between the fairways. Laid out on the Vergelegen Estate owned by the Gant family, the course was designed by Gary Player and his team of course designers in the mid-1990s.

Located at the foot of the impressive Helderberg mountains amid surrounding vineyards, it is divided into two distinctive nines. The first, built on the low-lying area within the suburbs of Somerset West, features fairly flat holes with some links-like characteristics such as undulating fairways, deep bunkers with sod faces, and few trees.

The back nine is built on the mountain slopes, affording glorious views of the Atlantic Ocean and False Bay across to the Cape Peninsula. Trees and water are much more in evidence here, giving it a parkland character. Much in evidence, too, is the wind that funnels down the mountain slopes to increase the difficulty of the fairly straightforward layout.

The par-five 13th is particularly dramatic. Played downhill and slightly to the left, it enjoys an impressive mountain backdrop with vines stretching into the distance. On a clear day, the view from the 15th tee is as stunning as one can hope to see from a golf course, but concentration must be maintained in order to negotiate this rather tricky par four. The 16th and 17th holes, played directly downhill back towards the clubhouse, are very exposed to the winds. The 17th, in particular, is a frightening prospect as the golfer is faced with the out-of-bounds fence on the right and trees on the left.

Shortly after the course was opened it played host to the 1996 World Cup of Golf – the first time the event had been played in South Africa. Dominated for the previous four years by the team of Davis Love III and Fred Couples from the USA, the 1996 event saw the USA team, this time comprising Tom Lehman and Steve Jones, hoping to win the cup for a record fifth time in succession.

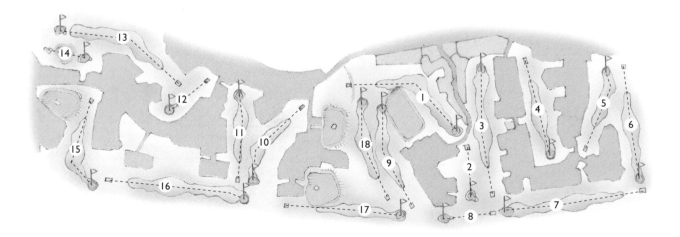

RIGHT: *The green of the par-three 8th which is played towards the picturesque Helderberg mountains. In the background is the green of the par-four 17th. The proximity to False Bay exposes the course to the Cape's notorious gale-force winds.*

But it was the South African team of Ernie Els and Wayne Westner who delighted their home crowds, romping to victory by several shots, while Els also picked up individual honours.

The course has since changed substantially in character, with more houses springing up as landowners comply with building deadlines. As the course matures and many of the young trees grow to full size, it will continue to be regarded as one of the finest and fairest tests of golf in the Cape.

ERINVALE
GARY PLAYER'S VIEW

I am proud to say that my golf course architecture team designed this unique course. As you play through the back nine holes, you climb dramatically up the mountain for a spectacular view of the Helderberg and Hottentots Holland mountains. The sea in the distance, and the many wineries for which the Cape is famous, including the Vergelegen winery right next to the course, are further attractions. Once all the trees mature, I think this will be one of the best golf courses in South Africa.

ABOVE: *Action during the 1996 World Cup of Golf on the 15th green. The event was won by South Africa's Ernie Els and Wayne Westner. In the background is the coastal town of Strand.*

ROYAL MELBOURNE

When East meets West

VICTORIA, AUSTRALIA

Royal Melbourne is one of the world's great championship courses outside the USA and the UK, an amalgamation of the work of two great golf course designers, Alex Russell and Dr Alister Mackenzie. The Royal Melbourne Golf Club was founded in 1891, a few years after golf spread to the southern hemisphere with the formation of Dunedin Golf Club in Otago, New Zealand, in 1871 and the Royal Cape Golf Club in Cape Town, South Africa, in 1885.

Membership of the Melbourne Club comprised many immigrants from the UK, some of whom hailed from the home of golf, St Andrews in Scotland. It was hardly surprising, then, that they sought out a stretch of heather-covered duneland very similar in appearance to Scottish linksland for the site of their new course in 1924. They imported a brilliant architect to design it, Alister Mackenzie, who had the wisdom to involve the current Australian Open champion, Alex Russell, as his partner in the design. Russell subsequently added a second course, and both courses were further refined by head green keeper, Claude Crockford, who deserves much of the credit for the lasting fame of Royal Melbourne. Holes from both courses make up the so-called Composite course, the selection partly governed by a road crossing. The result is a course of outstanding quality, with an intriguing mix of Augusta-like beauty and Scottish links-type characteristics. The course has earned a reputation for

what are undoubtedly among the world's fastest and truest greens, while its rough-hewn bunkers add to the severity of the challenge it poses.

In 1959, Royal Melbourne hosted the World Cup (then called the Canada Cup). Appropriately, it was won by the home team of Peter Thomson and Ken Nagle. It hosted the event again in 1972 when the Taiwanese team was the surprise winner. In 1998, Royal Melbourne hosted the Presidents Cup, played between an American and an International team. It was fitting that Peter Thomson should be the non-playing captain of the International team, with four Australians among the team members. They took on the much-favoured American team under captain Jack Nicklaus in what was the first Presidents Cup played outside the USA. The latter had won both previous encounters, in 1994 and 1996, at the Robert Trent Jones Golf

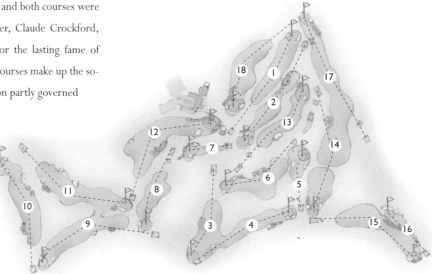

LEFT: *Royal Melbourne's 18-hole championship layout is an amalgamation of 12 holes from the East course and six holes from the West.*

ROYAL MELBOURNE

GARY PLAYER'S VIEW

Royal Melbourne's West and East courses are among the most famous in Australia, but it is the Composite course people refer to when ranking Royal Melbourne as one of the world's greatest. The East course has the fastest greens I have ever putted, and both courses are at times very windy. Royal Melbourne, famous for its large and dramatically-shaped bunkers, is as much a work of art as a playing field. Nowhere is this more apparent than on several par-four holes, with their daunting diagonal bunkers angling across the fairways. You have to keep the ball very straight as Mackenzie's mammoth sand bunkers can gobble up your ball in a flash.

Club in Virginia. Under a relentless Australian sun, on the second-hottest day in Melbourne that century, eight members of the TV crew collapsed, and the American team wilted. After four days and 32 matches on the 6392m (6981yd) par-72 layout, the International team emerged triumphant, scoring an emphatic $20\frac{1}{2}$ to $11\frac{1}{2}$ victory.

ABOVE: *Players make their way onto the green of Royal Melbourne's challenging par-four 18th during the 1991 Johnnie Walker Australian Classic. The green is guarded by large and unusually shaped bunkers.*

SAN LORENZO

Showpiece of the Algarve

QUINTA DO LAGO, AMANCIL, PORTUGAL

Since the 2000ha (4942 acres) Quinta do Lago estate on Portugal's Algarve coast derives its name from the large number of lakes on this piece of land, water is a significant factor at the estate's San Lorenzo golf course. Designed in 1988 by American golf course architects Joseph Lee and Rocky Roquemore, San Lorenzo also features abundant umbrella pine trees and offers fine views over the woodlands and wildlife of the Ria Formosa nature reserve from the 6th, 7th and 8th holes which run alongside it.

The par-72 San Lorenzo layout, rated 73 and measuring 6238m (6822yd), features several holes that require tactical planning. Water laps the edge of the fairway all the way to the green on the spectacular par-four 6th, while the 8th is a 525m (574yd) par five leading up to a huge lake where a slice will lead to a dropped shot. The 18th is particularly dramatic, featuring an island green that demands a calculated, accurate approach.

The Algarve is a popular holiday spot and a well-known golfing destination, but for golfers aspiring to play San Lorenzo, money and a bag of clubs may not be enough. This busy public course is often booked up by residents of a nearby hotel and green-fee players sometimes struggle to get a slot.

The greenkeeper's policy of preparing San Lorenzo as if for a new tournament every day ensures that its superbly manicured condition is maintained and its status as the showpiece of the Algarve is secure.

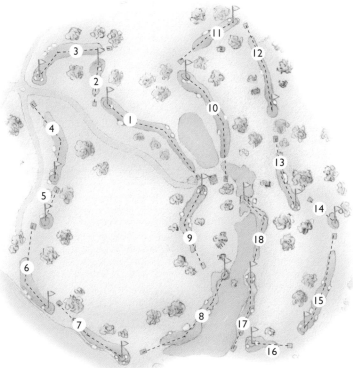

RIGHT: *San Lorenzo's par-four 6th hole offers spectacular views of the Ria Formosa nature reserve. Water runs along the right-hand side of the fairway all the way to the green. Similar views can be seen from the 7th and 8th holes as well.*

SAN LORENZO
GARY PLAYER'S VIEW

The Quinta do Lago development forms part of the National Park of Ria Formosa, a lovely park with mature woodlands and attractive lakes. The entire area is respected for its environmental stewardship. No two holes on this golf course are alike — the 5th offers marvellous views of the Atlantic Ocean, while the 8th faces the largest of the lakes. Visiting golfers have several world-class resort complexes from which to choose, including a five-star hotel.

ABOVE: *A large lake comes into play at San Lorenzo's finishing holes, the 17th and the formidable 18th. Tall umbrella pines line the course's perfectly manicured fairways.*

GOLF'S FINAL FRONTIERS

Pushing the barriers of nature

MODERN EARTH-MOVING MACHINERY AND VAST SUMS of money have allowed man to push aside nature's barriers and build golf courses in previously inhospitable environments. Desert, bushveld and mountain courses represent the breaching of golf's final frontier – a relatively new phenomenon because until recently it was impossible to build a golf course in an area without water, soil or trees, or on steep mountain slopes.

These classes of course are as much a triumph of advancing technology as they are of the skills and imagination of the golf course architects who create them – not to mention the size of the bank balances that fund them.

Desert golf courses, in particular, are a triumph. Presenting golfers with wide open spaces, perfectly maintained courses, year-round sunshine and spectacular vistas from the dry yellows and browns of the desert backdrop, they create a striking contrast with emerald-green expanses of fairways and greens. Gary Player's Egyptian creation at Soma Bay, in addition to a number of courses that have sprung up in the United Arab Emirates – like the Emirates Golf Club which now hosts events on the European Tour – and American courses such as Mission Hills in Palm Springs, have helped to put desert golf on the world map.

Mountain courses, such as Crans-sur-Sierre in Switzerland, offer some of the most spectacular views in world golf – vistas that have not been lost on the golfing public through the televising of the European Masters played there every year.

Bushveld courses are unique to the continent of Africa. South African layouts such as the Gary Player Country Club and Lost City Country Club at Sun City near Johannesburg, as well as Leopard Creek near the Kruger National Park, are cut out of the rugged African bush. Leopard Creek, in particular, provides golfers with unparalleled close-up views of

nature as wild animals freely roam the course. As golf has expanded around the world, golf course architects have been drawn by the spectacular views and variety of landscapes.

Ocean golf courses, such as Pebble Beach in California, are constructed on sites that cannot be classified as linksland although they are close to the sea, and they frequently contain elements of parkland courses when the layouts turn inland. When the layout runs close to the sea, however, they offer dramatic views and demanding shots, often played over high cliffs and crashing waves. Ocean courses, like links courses, are exposed to coastal winds that whip in off the sea and can instantly transform the character of the course.

A trend in modern golf course construction is towards 'stadium' courses – a phenomenon particularly popular in America. When designing these courses, the architects are at pains to create layout features that test golfers' skills, as well as to create enough space for spectators to view the action during big tournaments. As a result, high mounds are often found around tees and greens. Today, there are a number of **TPCs (Tournament Players Courses)** specifically designed to host professional events, including Gary Player's TPC at Jasna Polana in Princeton, New Jersey; the TPC at Sawgrass in Ponte Vedra Beach, Florida, which is the permanent home of the US PGA Tour's Players Championship; and the TPC at Summerlin, home of the Las Vegas Invitational.

While TPCs are designed specifically to host the world's best golfers under tournament conditions, **resort courses** are often designed with exactly the opposite in mind. They typically feature wide playing corridors, large greens and numerous tee options. Like TPCs, they are also a modern-day phenomenon, born out of the game's burgeoning popularity and the demand for playing facilities by golfers of all skill levels.

ABOVE: *The new par-three 5th hole at Pebble Beach, California, which was designed by Jack Nicklaus in 1997. The original 5th hole was routed inland through forest while the new hole takes golfers along the clifftops of the rugged Monterey Peninsula, affording dramatic views across Stillwater Cove and the Pacific Ocean.*

ABOVE: *Switzerland's Crans-sur-Sierre is among the most scenic tournament venues used on the European PGA Tour, hosting the annual European Masters.*

Under snow for the winter months when the practice tee becomes a beginner's ski-slope, the course returns to peak condition for the summer golfing season.

CYPRESS POINT

Wild beauty on Monterey Peninsula

PEBBLE BEACH, CALIFORNIA, USA

Cypress Point is an ocean layout of exceptional natural beauty, and a masterpiece of golf course design. Gary Player rates it as one of the world's most complete golf courses: 'Its terrain offers a hint of parkland that expands into a form of heathland and then a stretch of links by the sea, combining all forms of golf as we know it.'

Located 160km (100 miles) south of San Francisco, not far from its more famous neighbour, Pebble Beach, Cypress is situated in the foothills of the Santa Lucia mountains on the wild and rugged southern tip of the Monterey Peninsula. When the tide is out, the land drops in places some 20m (66ft) in a series of spectacular cliffs and, when the tide comes in, the huge waves of the Pacific Ocean pound the edge of the course.

Cypress Point is set within the Del Monte forest, and the fairways and some of the

greens are lined with the inescapable, brooding presence of the huge Monterey Cypresses that give the course its name. Wild deer roam the peninsula, sea lions bask in the sunlight on the rocks and fishing boats dot the wide blue ocean.

It was in this spectacular natural setting that famous golf course architect Dr Alister Mackenzie created his masterpiece in 1928. At no point was course quality sacrificed to take advantage of the natural beauty or majestic views, and the Scotsman built considerable slope and contour into the greens to compensate for the shortness of the course; it measures just 5949m (6506yd) from the championship tees. An unusual feature is the inclusion of both consecutive par fives and consecutive par threes. It also has all its par fives in the first 10 holes, and two par threes in the final four holes.

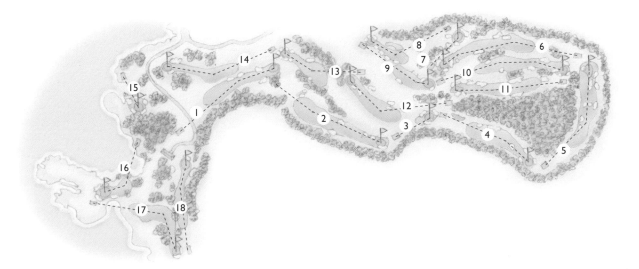

LEFT: *The 15th, 16th and 17th holes at Cypress Point are played along the clifftops of the Monterey Peninsula overlooking the Pacific Ocean. In the foreground is the green of the par-three 16th, which requires a carry of 213m (233yd) over the ocean.*

Undoubtedly the most spectacular hole on the course is the par-three 16th. The green and the tee are perched above the raging Pacific on either side of a cove, and the drive must carry the full 213m (233yd) over the water. Gary Player rates this as one of golf's most magical holes: 'The brave man bids for the green knowing full well the penalties of failure. His cautious opponent settles for a mid-iron along the clifftop with an outside hope of a chip and putt to save his par. It remains the classic example of strategic golf.'

When the hole is played into the teeth of the prevailing wind, it would be true to say that only the strongest of hitters can reach the green with an iron.

Despite its status, Cypress Point has never held a major championship and it remains one of the world's most exclusive golf clubs, with just 250 members.

For many years, Cypress Point was one of the courses used for the Bing Crosby National Pro-Am (along with Pebble Beach and Spyglass Hill). It brought together movie stars and pop singers, sporting celebrities and politicians, as well as the tour stars. Neighbouring Poppy Hills has taken its place.

CYPRESS POINT
GARY PLAYER'S VIEW

Cypress Point is one of my three favourite courses. If I had to play one course every single day, it would probably be this one. The layout is magnificent, requiring thought, not strength, to play it well. The tees are hidden in the long grasses, and I like that. The design is great, partly because it offers the golfer long holes as well as very good short par fours like the 8th and 9th holes. The 8th is a wonder, combining elements of Scotland, Pine Valley and the Monterey Peninsula. The 16th and 17th, where you must play directly over the Pacific Ocean, are thrilling holes to play.

TOP: *On the inland part of the course, the fairway of Cypress Point's par-four 11th is flanked by tall trees. Mackenzie's imaginative work here led to his being asked to collaborate with Bobby Jones on the creation of Augusta National.*

ABOVE: *The view from the 16th tee. The hole is played into the prevailing wind to a green surrounded by bunkers. Many players use the alternative route to the left, playing a drive and a pitch and settling for a bogey four.*

PEBBLE BEACH

Golf's most famous finishing holes

MONTEREY, CALIFORNIA, USA

Punched out into the Pacific Ocean by the Santa Lucia mountains on the south side of Monterey Bay, the Monterey Peninsula is home to three courses of the highest quality – Cypress Point, Spyglass Hill and Pebble Beach.

In 1914, Samuel Morse, nephew of the man who invented the telegraph, was sent to the Monterey Peninsula by the Southern Pacific Railroad Company to dispose of its real estate in the area. Recognizing the potential of the land, Morse bought some 2833ha (7000 acres) for US$1.3 million. Morse's company, Del Monte Property, sold the ground on which Cypress Point now stands for US$150,000. Convinced that a golf course would enhance the remaining land, he commissioned real-estate salesman Jack Neville to design and construct a golf course on part of it. Although not a golf course designer in the traditional sense, Neville was a fine golfer, having twice won the California State Championship, and it is difficult to believe that anyone could have bettered his design.

The opening holes run inland away from the sea, giving little hint of their later magic. The 3rd, a straightforward par four, runs west towards the sea and the next, a short par four, offers the first sight of the ocean.

Neville had wanted to build the par-three 5th hole along the clifftop, but Morse had sold that piece of land and the new owner could not be persuaded to sell. Only in 1997 did the Pebble Beach Company buy back the land and Jack Nicklaus was commissioned to design the new par-three 5th that now fronts the ocean as Neville had intended.

The par-four 8th rates as one of the most spectacular holes in world championship golf. At a length of 382m (418yd), it must be played carefully, driving along a plateau that borders the ocean. From there the second shot must be

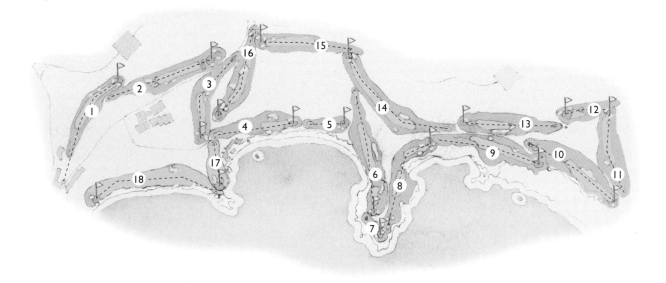

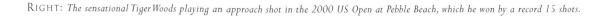

RIGHT: *The sensational Tiger Woods playing an approach shot in the 2000 US Open at Pebble Beach, which he won by a record 15 shots.*

his chip shot for birdie in the 1982 US Open Championship. At 190m (208yd), the 17th is dangerously long, and is played to a narrow green that is exposed to all the winds that blow off the bay. The 18th is a dramatic par five that runs along the rugged coastline, doglegging slightly to the left. Despite his emphatic record-breaking 15-shot margin in the 2000 US Open played at Pebble Beach, even Tiger Woods managed to find the ocean with his tee shot in the second round. Former PGA and Open champion, and bad-boy of golf, big-

played over a ravine towards the green some 150m (164yd) away. Care must be taken not to hit the drive too far, which makes for a tough choice of club off the tee.

The 17th and 18th are among the most famous finishing holes in golf, with many dramatic tournaments being decided on these holes. One of the most well-known images of modern Major championships is that of Tom Watson sinking

hitting John Daly, managed to find a way to crash to a nine over par 14 on this closing hole in the second round, proof perhaps that even the better golfers in the world can be brought to their knees by this course.

Pebble Beach is still a public facility, so anyone prepared to spend the US$ 350 green fee (making it the world's most expensive public course) can play there.

PEBBLE BEACH
GARY PLAYER'S VIEW

This shrine of American golf is a dream everybody has to play sometime or another. Pebble Beach has it all: great elevation changes; small, subtle greens; inland holes; ocean holes; and a setting as breathtakingly beautiful as anywhere on earth. Great golf courses seem to have an uncanny way of producing wonderful golf tournaments, with unforgettable shots and world-class champions. Who can forget Jack Nicklaus's one-iron shot on the par-three 17th in 1972, which hit the pin to secure him the US Open title? Or, 10 years later, Tom Watson's miraculous chip shot from the rough alongside the same green to beat Jack Nicklaus?

ABOVE: *Tom Watson plays during the 1982 US Open at Pebble Beach. His triumph is best remembered for his chip-in birdie at the 17th to snatch victory from arch-rival Jack Nicklaus.*

RIGHT: *Perched on the peninsula that forms one side of Stillwater Cove, the par-three 7th hole is typical of the dramatic clifftop layout of Pebble Beach.*

RIA BINTAN

Between the forest and the South China Sea

RIA BINTAN RESORT, BINTAN, INDONESIA

The island of Bintan in Indonesia, just 45 minutes' ferry ride from Singapore's Tanah Merah Ferry Terminal, is home to one of Asia's most scenic ocean golf courses. The 27-hole Ria Bintan golf course meanders through serene tropical forest and along the South China Sea, providing golfers with breathtaking scenery and an exhilarating golfing experience. Apart from the course's striking natural elements, it is the bunkering that adds to its dramatic appeal. Sharp, steep faces, often cast in shadows, contrast with the white sand, luxuriously manicured greens, heavily wooded backdrops and churning sea.

Early in 1994, Keppel Land commissioned Gary Player to create a championship golf course. Player set to work on a piece of land he described as 'one of the best sites I have worked with anywhere in the world'.

The Ria Bintan golf course opened for play in late 1998, an important component of a 447ha (1105 acres) resort that is a joint venture between the governments of Singapore and Indonesia. It will eventually include various hotels, resort homes, seaside villas and condominiums, as well as a Club Med Holiday Resort.

The course's most spectacular hole is undoubtedly the par-three 9th, one of Asia's best short holes. The green is situated on a rocky outcrop that juts into the ocean, while cascading rocks have been used to form the platform for the green. Natural rainforest provides a backdrop to the long but very narrow putting surface – a distant target when the wind is blowing from the east. The 18th, a 445m (487yd) dogleg-left par four, with water to the left and dense forest to the right, is one of Asia's toughest finishing holes. A well-struck tee shot should find the generous landing area but the approach shot to the green must contend with a massive lake that extends right up to the putting surface.

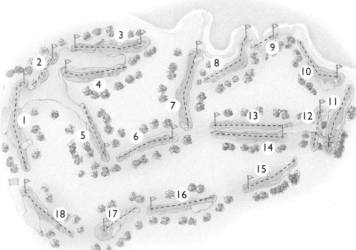

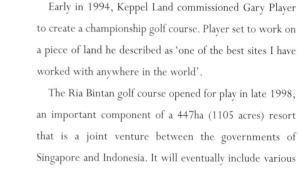

LEFT: *Ria Bintan's 10th hole is a flat par four that doglegs left, following the coastline, to a large undulating green guarded by pot bunkers.*

RIA BINTAN

GARY PLAYER'S VIEW

This course, over 6400m (7000yd) long, has five sets of tees to accommodate all levels of skill. It is built amongst heavy bush on the sea's edge, with one green literally on rocks right out in the ocean. It is as fine a layout and as great a golfing experience as you can find, in its own way rivalling the magnificent Pebble Beach. With its magnificent clubhouse through which the fresh sea-air breezes, it is probably the best course in Indonesia.

TOP: *Towering pines flank the fairway of Ria Bintan's par-five 7th as it winds down towards the ocean, providing golfers with their first good view of the coastline. With water to the right of the green and sand protecting the left, a lay-up shot would be the first choice for most sensible golfers.*

ABOVE: *The 9th is regarded as one of Asia's most magnificent par threes. Tumbling boulders create a platform for the long and narrow putting surface extending into the ocean, backed by tall palms and verdant greenery.*

GARY PLAYER COUNTRY CLUB

Carved out of the African bush

SUN CITY, SOUTH AFRICA

The Gary Player Country Club was the first course constructed at the famous Sun City resort in South Africa in the late 1970s. Although it is essentially a resort course, Player was given the brief to create a course that would test the very best golfers in the world in the Million Dollar Golf Challenge, now renamed the Nedbank Golf Challenge.

'What a golf course needs is elasticity, not simply to accommodate the long hitters, but in displaying a variety of tees with bunkers designed to challenge them,' says Player. 'Thus a golf course must be all things to all men. It must be flexible enough to provide a varying challenge for the old lady golfer, the young player and the top professional.'

Player introduced some of the most modern design features into the layout: large, clover-shaped and severely contoured greens, substantial mounds into which bunkers were cut, and multiple tee positions. The latter innovation, particularly, makes the course accessible to golfers of

all skill levels. To the Nedbank Challenge pros, the course is a stern test, yet it presents plenty of birdie and eagle opportunities for those willing and able to rise to the 'risk and reward' challenge of Player's layout.

This philosophy is nowhere more apparent than at the par-five 9th, the course's signature hole. 'The 9th can be classified as a heroic par five, even though it is regularly set up to allow players to reach the green on their second shot. This is a hole where a swing of two or three shots can occur,' says Player. The hole has just one bunker – on the right and in the landing area of the tee shot. The fairway then curves left to a spectacular island green rising out of a dam with Sun City as a backdrop.

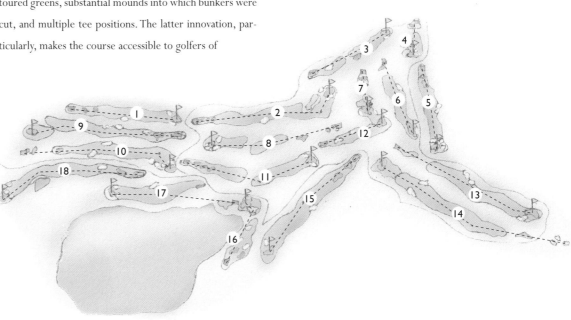

LEFT: *The green of the par-three 16th at the Gary Player Country Club slopes sharply upwards from front to back, which varies the difficulty of the hole substantially depending on the chosen pin position.*

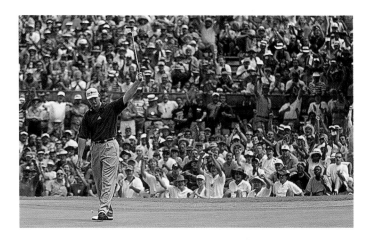

Golfers can play safe by laying up in front of the water and reaching the green in three; or they can attempt to reach the green in two for an eagle opportunity, but with a greater risk of putting it in the water.

The layout measures a daunting 7033m (7691yd) from the championship tees, providing a test worthy of the world's best, and the annual Million Dollar Challenge has grown to become Southern Africa's biggest golfing event, televised around the world. The winners read like a who's who of world golf, including superstars Johnny Miller (who won the inaugural event in 1981), Seve Ballesteros, Bernhard Langer, Nick Faldo, Nick Price, Mark McNulty, Fulton Allem, Ernie Els and Colin Montgomerie. Keeping abreast of the huge influx of money into tournament golf, from 2000 the Nedbank Golf Challenge offers an unprecedented US$2 million first prize to the victor.

The course constantly undergoes small design and construction changes to keep up with modern trends in golf course design. One is the bunker that has been added to the tough par-four finishing hole on the right of the fairway. The hole requires an accurate drive up the left side of the fairway but, because it is flanked by water, the right-hand side has always been the safe side. The hole then turns sharply to the left with the long-iron approach being played across water to a slightly raised green. The bunker now catches the conservative drive down the right, leaving the golfer a desperately difficult shot to the green.

An important aspect of Gary Player's golf course design philosophy is that the course should enhance the environment. Only indigenous trees have been planted, the roads are dirt, natural stone has been used for retaining walls and walkways, and the rough bordering the fairways is thick, virgin bush.

Out on the course, far from the hustle and bustle of the resort and surrounded on all sides by tall trees and the peaks of the Pilanesberg hills that form the rim of an ancient volcanic crater, one can truly appreciate the tranquillity of African bushveld and the unique setting of this remarkable golf course.

GARY PLAYER
GARY PLAYER'S VIEW

Because it bears my name, this course is one of the more special courses on which I have worked. It is probably the second toughest golf course in Southern Africa, although the Million Dollar Challenge has never been played when it was set up very hard. When it is, it could easily be the toughest course in the world. The golfer must drive the ball very accurately to be in the proper position to play difficult approach shots to the contoured greens. This course really captures the spirit of golf in Africa, allowing golfers to enjoy the atmosphere of adventure with baboons, deer and other passers-by who 'share' the course with them.

ABOVE LEFT: *South Africa's Ernie Els celebrates as his eagle putt drops on the par-five 9th hole during the 1999 Nedbank Golf Challenge. Els went on to win the event for the first time.*

BELOW: *The spectacular island green of the par-five 9th at the Gary Player Country Club.*

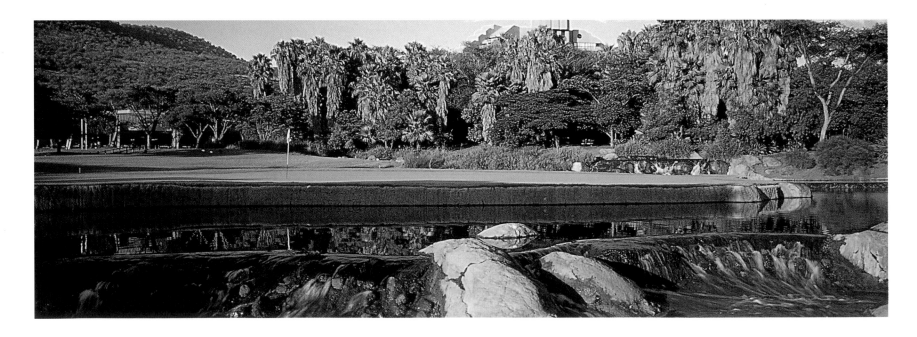

THE LOST CITY

Crocodiles in the water hazard

SUN CITY, SOUTH AFRICA

South Africa's Lost City Country Club offers an extraordinary 'African' golfing experience on one of the toughest courses in the country.

The course was built in 1992 at the Sun City complex northwest of Johannesburg, a world-famous resort best known to golfers for hosting the Million Dollar Challenge, now renamed the Nedbank Golf Challenge.

Like its better-known 'sister' nearby, the Gary Player Country Club, The Lost City course was designed by Gary Player, although in substantially different style. As it opened 13 years after the Gary Player Country Club, when golf buggies had become commonplace, the Gary Player design team could increase the distance between greens and tees. As a result, especially on the second

nine, Player could make use of view-site tees high on the slopes of the surrounding hills. The course has two distinctly different nines, the first being relatively flat with an obvious desert-like aspect. There are a number of large waste-bunkers (which, unlike traditional bunkers, are not raked) featuring a variety of cacti, and the fairways have generous landing areas in keeping with the resort nature of the facility.

The second nine, by contrast, has more elevated tees, and the stretch from the 14th to the 16th holes has features of a classic bushveld layout: tighter fairways and lush foliage surrounding the dramatic holes.

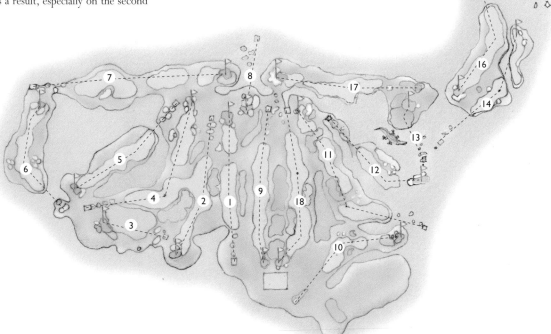

RIGHT: *The water hazard short of the par-five 18th's green. In the background is the unusual clubhouse, built according to the 'ruins' theme of The Lost City. The annual Dimension Data Pro-Am on the Southern Africa Tour is played on both layouts at Sun City.*

At some 475m (520yd) from the professionals' tee, the 9th hole is one of the longest par fours to be found anywhere in the world, although the course's multiple tees allow those unable to cope with such vast distances to play the hole considerably shorter. The short 13th has an unusual water hazard inhabited by a number of fairly hungry-looking crocodiles which make retrieving a wayward shot rather unwise.

The unique clubhouse is built along the same theme as The Lost Palace hotel – that of a ruined city 'discovered' after centuries of mystery. It overlooks both the 9th and 18th holes and gives spectacular views of most of the front nine.

The grass on all the fairways has recently been replaced with Kikuyu which has ensured a better playing surface throughout the year in what can be a very harsh climate, especially in mid-summer.

With the abundance of bird and wildlife on the course, it offers the visitor a truly 'African' experience as well as a golfing experience matched by few.

THE LOST CITY
GARY PLAYER'S VIEW

One of my favourite courses in South Africa, The Lost City was carved out of the African bush. A very strategic layout, it requires the best shot-making of any golf course in South Africa. Big tees, set high in the hills with massive rocks in a desert-style theme, make it unique. The par-three 13th, with crocodiles on the edge of the green, provides an incredible golfing experience, while the bunkers around this green display three different colours of sand – a gesture that celebrates the multiracial make-up of my country.

RIGHT: *A view from the 17th green up the par-five finishing hole towards the clubhouse. On the left is the spectacular and exclusive hotel — the Palace of The Lost City.*

LEOPARD CREEK

An 'African' Augusta

MALELANE, MPUMALANGA, SOUTH AFRICA

On the southern border of South Africa's Kruger National Park, near Malelane, is Leopard Creek Country Club, one of the country's finest and most exclusive golfing venues. Business magnate and golfing benefactor, Johann Rupert, enlisted the skills of Gary Player in 1994 to construct what he envisaged as an 'African' Augusta. In a no-expense-spared project, Player was instructed simply to 'build the best course in Africa'.

Rupert found in Player a kindred spirit: they share a deep love of golf as well as of the African bush. Completed in 1996, this golf course is magnificent in terms of the quality of the challenge it presents to golfers, the conditioning of the layout, and the way it blends with and enhances the natural environment. As it is set in the rugged wilderness of the Mpumalanga bushveld, sightings of crocodile, hippopotamus, wild pig, buffalo, elephant and various species of antelope are common, especially around the many watercourses and the Crocodile River that runs alongside three holes. The indigenous trees and bush on the course are also home to over 200 species of birds.

Creating and maintaining a championship-quality golf course in the middle of the African bushveld is no small task. Over 35ha (86 acres) of ground are under lush Kikuyu grass, but the original area had little topsoil and was covered in rock. A rock-picker was brought in to clear the land and 55,000m³ (1.9 million ft³) of topsoil were laid down to ensure a good base for the turf. Fine white bunker sand was trucked in from Bronkhorstspruit to cover the more than 1ha (2.5 acres) of bunkering, forming an attractive contrast with the green Kikuyu. To irrigate and maintain the grass, huge storage dams were constructed and an irrigation system was installed with over 1200 sprinkler heads, capable of pumping over three million litres (660,000 gal) of water a day onto the course.

Water features and dams form an integral part of the Leopard Creek layout, and the course's magnificent clubhouse looks out over the 9th and 18th greens, which share a common water hazard.

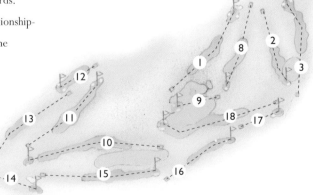

LEFT: *The view down the 10th hole from the clubhouse at Leopard Creek shows the lush green fairways, which contrast strongly with the rugged African bushveld. A statue of a leopard marks the tee at each hole on the course.*

LEOPARD CREEK

GARY PLAYER'S VIEW

Leopard Creek is surrounded by bushveld. The fact that you could be playing while hearing a hippopotamus snort or seeing a lion near the fence is unique, as is the pitch shot you might hit over a lake full of crocodiles and hippos. The clubhouse, an extraordinary piece of architecture with a thatch roof, is filled with golfing memorabilia. Just three years after its completion in 1996, Leopard Creek hosted a Shell's Wonderful World of Golf match between Ernie Els and Nick Price.

The peninsula green of the 9th hole is in fact completely surrounded by water, which is home to a number of hippos and crocodiles. The signature hole on the course is the 510m (558yd) par-five 4th. Situated on the banks of the Crocodile River, the green offers excellent views upriver where elephant can often be seen.

Virgin bush flanks the lush Kikuyu fairways, while stone walls and Scottish-style sod bunkers are a common feature. Each tee is marked with a unique statue of a leopard, serving as a constant reminder that one is playing in the heart of the African bush.

Leopard Creek is an exclusive venue. On a private golf estate with only 200 lodges, the course is only accessible to members and their guests, or residents at a nearby resort.

ABOVE: The 9th and 18th greens at Leopard Creek share a common water hazard, one that is home to a number of hippos and crocodiles. The fairways of these holes run parallel towards the greens situated in front of the magnificent thatched clubhouse.

CRANS-SUR-SIERRE
Golf in the Swiss Alps

MONTANA, SWITZERLAND

Crans-sur-Sierre, set high on a mountain plateau above the Rhône Valley in Switzerland's Berner Alps, must rank as one of the world's most spectacularly scenic golf courses. Each year in late August or early September, golfers on the European Tour gather in the shadow of the majestic, snowcapped peaks of the Alps and the rugged silhouette of the Matterhorn to play in one of Europe's oldest and most prestigious events: the Canon European Masters. Previously known as the Swiss Open, the event has been played here since 1939. Popular and worthy winners over the years have included the Spaniards Seve Ballesteros (in 1977, 1978 and 1989) and José Maria Olazábal (1986), Scot Colin Montgomerie (1996), Italian Costantino Rocca (1997) and Englishman Lee Westwood (1999).

Three-time winner Ballesteros is still fondly remembered for his miraculous recovery shot in the 1993 event, a feat commemorated by a plaque deep in the undergrowth near the 18th fairway.

Ballesteros has a further interest in this golf course: together with the design team of his Trajectory Golf Course Design company, he has modified and redesigned all 18 holes at Crans-sur-Sierre.

Crans-sur-Sierre's altitude, 1600m (4390ft) above sea level, means that the 6165m (6744yd) par-71 course is shortened by the greater distances the ball

flies in the rarefied air. This has allowed several European Tour records to be set here, most notably an 18-hole record of 60 by Italian Baldovino Dassu in the 1961 Swiss Open, and a nine-hole record of 27 by Olazábal in the 1978 Open.

Although skiing holiday pioneer Sir Arnold Lunn opened a golf course here in 1905, the sport did not prove popular among the region's tourists who preferred the pistes to the fairways, and it closed during World War I. The course was successfully reopened in 1927, and golf has grown in popularity in the area ever since, spurred by the hosting of the annual Swiss Open.

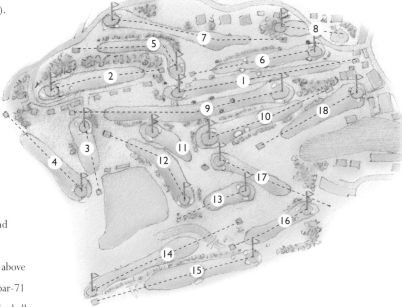

RIGHT: *The snowcapped peaks of the Swiss Alps form a spectacular backdrop to the green of the short par-four 7th hole at Crans-sur-Sierre.*

CRANS-SUR-SIERRE
GARY PLAYER'S VIEW

Crans-sur-Sierre is a true golf and outdoor paradise. Greg Norman once told the organizers of
the European Masters that they had 'the most
spectacular tournament course in the world' –
high praise from a man like Norman who has
played golf around the globe. I have always
enjoyed visiting the Crans-sur-Sierre course:
the hotel accommodation and the food are
wonderful and the atmosphere is so peaceful.
Here, golfers have the opportunity of playing
golf in the middle of the summer, with snowcapped mountains all around and an average
temperature of 20°C (68°F).

ABOVE: Swiss-style chalets overlook the green of Crans-sur
Sierre's par-four 4th hole. Measuring 456m (499yd), it is the
longest and most demanding par four on the course.

EMIRATES

Oasis in a sea of sand

MAJLIS COURSE, DUBAI, UNITED ARAB EMIRATES

Situated just outside the thriving trading and holiday centre of Dubai in the United Arab Emirates, the Emirates Golf Club was the first all-grass golf course to be constructed in the deserts of the Middle East.

The brainchild of Sheikh Mohammed bin Rashid Al Maktoum of Dubai's ruling family, the championship Majlis course was opened for play in 1988. Designed by American Karl Litten, it measures around 6584m (7200yd) and features many raised greens that add to its total length. The layout is generally tight requiring long, accurate tee shots, with the punishing rough made up of sandy desert and indigenous shrubs. The back nine features three par fives, two of which start or complete the loop. The par threes are fairly straightforward, while most of the par fours are taxing because of their length and awkward tee shots. As it is in the middle of the desert where daytime temperatures range from 30–49°C (89–120°F), nearly 4.5 million litres (990,000 gal) of water must be pumped on to the course through more than 500 sprinkler heads every day. An anomaly is that freshwater hazards on the course are plentiful, thanks mainly to the nearby aluminium factory with its adjoining water-desalination plant.

Emirates Golf Club is famous for its unique clubhouse, a towering construction designed in the shape of a Bedouin tent. Overlooking the 8th and 2nd greens, and 9th and 13th tees, is the similarly designed Royal Pavilion, the private entertainment centre for the Dubai ruling family's VIP guests at tournaments.

Until recently the Emirates Golf Club course has been home to the popular European Tour event, the Dubai Desert Classic, winners of which have included Ernie Els and former European Ryder Cup captains Seve Ballesteros and Mark James. In recent years the event has moved to

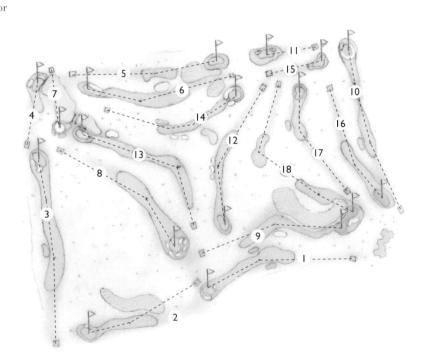

LEFT: *The holes on the Majlis championship course at Emirates Golf Club are typically surrounded by palm trees and many man-made bunkers. In the background can be seen the desert waste areas that line a few of the holes in stark contrast to the lush green of the fairways.*

another of Dubai's world-class facilities, the Dubai Creek Golf & Yacht Club.

A second 18-hole course has been added to the Majlis course at Emirates Golf Club. The Wadi course is built around the perimeter of the original Majlis course and incorporates another three 'Academy' holes, a popular addition to the club's practice facilities.

Dubai itself has become the playground of the Middle East, catering to the surrounding Arab population as well as to visitors from further afield. It is as well known today for sporting events like horse and camel racing as it is for its shopping festivals.

EMIRATES
GARY PLAYER'S VIEW

It is extraordinary to think that a grass course of the quality of this one was built on such a harsh desert landscape. Of course it would not have been possible without the amazing and very expensive engineering achievement of bringing desalinated water to the course to be used for irrigation. Dubai is fascinating and, for Westerners, an exotic place to visit. This is perhaps why the European Tour has made the Dubai Open a regular stop on its yearly schedule.

ABOVE: *The greens of the 9th and 18th are overlooked by the luxurious clubhouse with its unique design inspired by the shapes of Bedouin tents.*

THE CASCADES

Red Sea treasure

SOMA BAY, HURGHADA, EGYPT

The Gary Player-designed golf course at the Cascades Golf Resort and Country Club at Soma Bay is in many ways a first for Egypt. It is the first golf course opened for play on the west coast of the Red Sea and the first championship golf course in the Middle East designed by one of the 'Big Three' – Gary Player, Jack Nicklaus and Arnold Palmer.

This 18-hole, par-72 golf course offers spectacular views, both of lush green fairways that contrast dramatically with the starkness of the desert, and of the Red Sea, as several holes are located directly on the coast, with one green, the spectacular par-three 5th, actually jutting out into the sea.

The course was completed in November 1999 and Player described it at its inaugural event, the Cascades/Austrian Airlines Invitational Tournament, as 'the next Pebble Beach'.

Although this is a desert course, Player has brought water into play on several holes, using lakes, streams and the surrounding sea. Both the 9th and 18th holes finish in front of an imposing waterfall and the first of a series of cascading lakes after which the golf course is named.

One of the advantages of desert courses is that the weather is usually ideal for golf, and Soma Bay is no excep-

tion. The region has 360 days of sunshine a year and perfect temperatures for golf in winter – steady at around 25°C (77°F) – although it warms up in summer to around 35°C (95°F). The course is rendered more challenging by the vagaries of the coastal winds, but where else can one play a round of golf, scuba dive in the Red Sea, or visit the Great Pyramids just an hour's flight away?

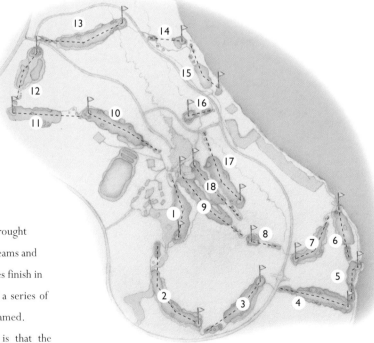

THE CASCADES
GARY PLAYER'S VIEW

This course stands on what was once a military base attacked on several occasions by the Israelis, and there were land mines that had to be removed before we began construction. Once a simple fishing village, Hurghada has become one of Egypt's top tourist spots, with its piercingly clear water, exotic reefs, many shipwrecks and some of the world's best scuba diving. Not only does this course have spectacular holes and scenery, it also offers golfers the experience of playing very close to the Red Sea, with a wealth of religious and cultural history right at their feet.

LEFT TOP: *The lush Kikuyu fairways provide a stark contrast to the large waste areas situated between the tees and fairways, and to the side of the fairways, at the Cascades golf course. The overall layout uses less than 30ha (74 acres) of irrigated turf.*

LEFT BOTTOM: *The spectacular par-three 5th hole is played over rocks, coral and water to a green jutting out into the Red Sea.*

ABOVE: *Four holes are situated directly at the Red Sea, and breezes off the water can become a significant element in the playing strategy of the course.*

MISSION HILLS NORTH

A splash of green in the California desert

PALM SPRINGS, CALIFORNIA, USA

Under the wide blue skies of California, in the shadow of the barren and rocky mountains that tower over the dry plains of Palm Springs, lies the first Gary Player-designed desert golf course.

Player rose admirably to the unique challenges he encountered during the construction of this, his first desert course at the Westin Mission Hills Resort. Millions of dollars were spent sculpting the dry Palm Springs earth into an impressive landscape featuring lush Bermuda grass covering the fairways, tees and greens, as well as several lakes, four waterfalls and over 2500 trees, Oleanders and indigenous plants. Over 6000 tonnes of natural and artificial rock were used in the construction of the course's extensive water hazards.

Completed in 1992, the Mission Hills North golf course is one of two 18-hole layouts at the resort. Measuring 6458m (7062yd) off the back tees with a par of 72, Mission Hills North is a long course, and the use of extensive bunkering, multi-levelled or elevated greens, mounding, narrow fairways and water features on many holes make it a stern test. Nevertheless, the golfer is rewarded by a golf course that is both challenging and fair, with excellent views of the surrounding countryside.

The Westin Mission Hills Resort was named as one of *Golf Magazine USA's* Silver Medal Resorts in 1996. The magazine also voted the course layout one of the top 10 new resort courses in the USA, a fitting tribute to Gary Player's vision, imagination and design skills.

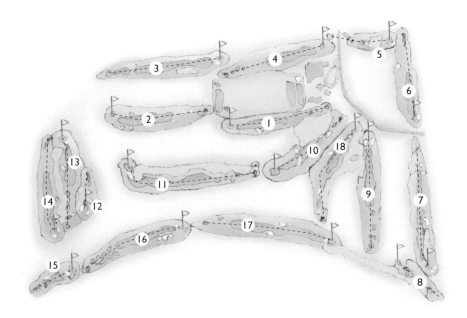

RIGHT: *Snowcapped peaks tower over the lush fairway and green of the 9th hole at Mission Hills North. This long par four is rated as the most difficult hole on the course. Mission Hills North hosts the LPGA's annual Nabisco Championship.*

MISSION HILLS NORTH

GARY PLAYER'S VIEW

The Mission Hills championship golf course hosts the LPGA's Nabisco Championship, formerly the Dinah Shore Nabisco Championship, each spring, and the television broadcast of that event has made this layout a familiar name to golf fans around the world. It is a lushly irrigated course carved out of the sand in the desert. Because of the water available to it from an underground source, the course is unusual in that it resembles a wooded parkland layout in the desert. Its many large water hazards, some with big boulders placed in the middle of the water, contribute to a memorable experience on an elegant course.

Years ago, you could find Johnny Revolta, a top player during the late 1930s, teaching on the practice tee at Mission Hills. 'Ring that bell!' he used to tell his students, meaning: finish with your hands nice and high, as if you were going to bang them into a bell up between your forward shoulder and your ear. Still good advice.

ABOVE: *Water plays a significant role at the Gary Player-designed Mission Hills North with lakes, streams and waterfalls coming into play on many of the holes.*

LINKS AND LINKS-LIKE COURSES

COURSE	CONTACT DETAILS	TYPE OF COURSE	OTHER COURSES NEARBY	NEAREST TOWN
St Andrews (Old)	Tel: (1334) 46-6666 Fax: (1334) 46-6664	Public	New course, Eden course, Balgove nine-hole course, Jubilee course, Strathtyrum course	St Andrews, Scotland
Royal Dornoch	Tel: (1862) 81-0219	Public	Struie course	Dornoch, Scotland
Ballybunion	Tel: (68) 2-7146 Fax: (68) 2-7387	Private	Cashen course	Ballybunion, Ireland
Carnoustie	Tel: (1241) 85-3789	Public	Buddon links, Burnside	Carnoustie, Scotland
Muirfield	Tel: (1620) 84-2123	Private	Gullane GC (courses 1, 2, 3), North Berwick West links, Whitekirk GC	Gullane, Scotland
Royal Troon	Tel: (1292) 31-1555 Fax: (1292) 31-8204	Private	Turnberry GC (Ailsa and Arran courses), Prestwick GC	Troon, Scotland
Turnberry (Ailsa)	Tel: (1655) 33-1000	Public	Arran course, Prestwick GC, Royal Troon GC	Turnberry and Glasgow, Scotland
Royal Birkdale	Tel: (1704) 56-9913	Private	Southport GC, Ainsdale GC	Southport, England
Royal Lytham	Tel: (1253) 72-0094	Private	St Annes Old Links GC	Blackpool, England
Royal St George's	Tel: (1304) 61-3090	Private	Royal Cinque Ports GC, Prince's GC	Sandwich, England
Portmarnock	Tel: (1) 846-2968	Private	Portmarnock links	Dublin, Ireland
Royal Country Down	Tel: (28437) 2-3314	Private	Second course	Newcastle, Northern Ireland
Royal Portrush	Tel: (2870) 82-2311 Fax: (2870) 82-3139	Private	Valley course	Portrush, Northern Ireland
Shinnecock Hills	Tel: (516) 283-3525	Private	National GC of America, Southampton GC	Southampton, New York, USA
Raspberry Falls	Tel: (703) 779-8721	Public	Lansdowne Resort, Westpark GC	Leesburg, USA
Seminole	Tel: (407) 626-0280	Private	Lost Tree GC, North Palm Beach CC	North Palm Beach, USA
Links at Fancourt	Tel: (44) 870-8282 Fax: (44) 870-7605	Public	Outeniqua and Montague courses at Fancourt, George Golf Club	George, South Africa
Noordwijk	Tel: (252) 37-0044	Private	Haagsche GC	Noordwijk, Holland
Sand River	Tel: (755) 690-0111 Fax: (755) 660-8687	Public	Shenzhen GC	Shenzhen, China
Kau Sai Chai	North course: Tel: (2) 791-3380 South course: Tel: (2) 791-3390 Fax: (2) 791-7293	Public	Hong Kong GC	Hong Kong

PARKLAND COURSES

COURSE	CONTACT DETAILS	TYPE OF COURSE	OTHER COURSES NEARBY	NEAREST TOWN
Augusta National	Tel/Fax: (706) 667-6000	Private	Augusta GC, August CC, Forest Hills GC	Augusta, USA
Cougar Point	Tel: (843) 76-82121 Fax: (843) 76-82726	Resort	Turtle Point course, Osprey Point course, Ocean course, Oak Point course	Kiawah Island, USA
Diamond Run	Tel: (412) 741-2582	Private	Allegheny CC	Pittsburgh, USA
Inverness	Tel: (419) 578-9000	Private	Ottawa Park GC, Heather Downs GC, South Toledo GC	Toledo, USA
Manhattan Woods	Tel: (914) 627-2222 Fax: (914) 627-0093	Private	Blue Hill GC, Spook Rock GC	West Nyack, New York, USA
Medinah	Tel: (708) 773-1700	Private	Second, Third courses	Chicago, USA
Oakmont	Tel: (412) 828-4653	Private	Oakmont East, Green Oaks CC, Fox Chapel GC	Oakmont, USA
Pine Valley	Tel: (856) 783-3000	Private	Valleybrook GC, Wedgewood CC	Clementon, USA
Floridian	Tel: (561) 781-1000	Private	Golden Bear GC at Hammond Creek	Palm City, USA
TPC at Jasna Polana	Tel: (609) 688-0500 Fax: (609) 924-0547	Private	Princeton CC, Bunker Hill GC	Princeton, USA
Oakland Hills (South)	Tel: (248) 644-2500	Private	North course, Birmingham CC	Detroit, USA
Winged Foot (West)	Tel: (914) 381-5821	Private	East course, Hampshire CC	Mamaroneck, USA
Pinehurst No. 2	Tel: (910) 295-8141 Fax: (910) 295-8111	Semi-private	Seven other courses at Pinehurst (Nos 1, 3, 4, 5, 6, 7, 8)	Pinehurst, USA
Congressional (Blue)	Tel: (301) 469-2032 Fax: (301) 469-2318	Private	Gold course, TPC at Avenel	Bethesda, USA
Wentworth	Tel: (1344) 84-2201 Fax: (1344) 84-2804	Public	East course, par three course, Sunningdale GC	Virginia Water, England
Five Nations	Tel: (8) 632-3232 Fax: (8) 632-3011	Private	Royal Golf des Fagnes Club, Royal GC du Sart Tilman	Méan, Belgium
Chantilly	Tel: (3) 4458-4774	Private	Nine-hole course	Chantilly, France
Sporting Club Berlin	Tel: (33631) 5268 Fax: (33631) 5270	Resort	Arnold Palmer course, Bernhard Langer course	Bad Saarow, Germany
Club zur Vahr	Tel: (421) 20-4480 Fax: (421) 244-9248	Private	Bremen course (nine holes)	Garlstadt, Germany
El Saler	Tel: (96) 161-1186 Fax: (96) 162-7016	Public	El Bosque GC, Manises GC	Valencia, Spain
Valderrama	Tel: (56) 79-6430 Fax: (56) 79-6431	Semi-private	Sotogrande, La Duquesa, Alcaidesa, San Roque	Sotogrande, Spain
Manna	Tel: (47) 524-5211 Fax: (47) 524-5218	Private	27-hole course at Country Club	Chiba, Japan
Erinvale	Tel: (21) 847-1144 Fax: (21) 847-1070	Private	Somerset West GC, Strand GC	Cape Town, South Africa
Royal Melbourne	Tel: (3) 9 598-6755 Fax: (3) 9 521-0065	Private	East and West courses	Melbourne, Australia
San Lorenzo	Tel: (89) 39-6522 Fax: (89) 39-6908	Resort/public	Quinta do Lago, Old Course, Ria Formosa	Quinta do Lago, Portugal

OCEAN, BUSHVELD, MOUNTAIN AND DESERT COURSES

COURSE	CONTACT DETAILS	TYPE OF COURSE	OTHER COURSES NEARBY	NEAREST TOWN
Cypress Point	Tel: (831) 624-2223 Fax: (831) 624-5057	Private	Pebble Beach, Spyglass Hill	Pebble Beach, USA
Pebble Beach	Tel: (831) 624-3811 Fax: (831) 622-8795	Public	Cypress Point, Spyglass Hill	Pebble Beach, USA
Ria Bintan	Tel: (770) 69-2868 Fax: (770) 69-2837	Resort	Forest course	Bintan, Indonesia
Gary Player CC	Tel: (14) 657-1020 Fax: (14) 657-3442	Public	The Lost City CC	Rustenburg, South Africa
Lost City	Tel: (14) 657-3700 Fax: (14) 657-3426	Public	Gary Player CC	Rustenburg, South Africa
Leopard Creek	Tel: (13) 790-3322	Private	Nelspruit GC, White River GC, Sabi River Sun	Malelane, South Africa
Crans sur Sierre	Tel: (27) 41-2168 or 41-2703 Fax: (27) 41-4671 or 41-9568	Private/Resort	Jack Nicklaus (nine holes), Super-Crans (nine holes), Sion GC	Montana, Switzerland
Emirates	Tel: (9714) 48-0222 Fax: (9714) 48-1888	Private	Wadi course, Dubai Creek, Dubai CC, Racing Club course	Dubai, United Arab Emirates
Cascades	Tel/Fax: (65) 54-4901	Resort	None	Hurghada, Egypt
Mission Hills	Tel: (800) 358-2211	Resort	Mission Hills CC, Arnold Palmer course, Pete Dye course	Rancho Mirage, USA

AUTHORS' ACKNOWLEDGMENTS

The authors would like to acknowledge the invaluable contributions and input of Andy Brumer of the Gary Player Group and Bernard Mostert of *Compleat Golfer* magazine, as well as the assistance and support of Beatrix Geen of the Gary Player Group, and the patience and superb editing skills of Roxanne Reid.

PHOTOGRAPHIC CREDITS

The copyright © of the photographs rests with the following photographers and/or their agents.   Touchline/Allsport = **T/A**

Richard J Castka, 64–65, 66, 140; **Cougar Point**, 74, 75 (right, left); **Peter Dazeley**, 19, 42 (bottom left), 43, 110 (top left); **Five Nations**, 111, 112; **courtesy of The Floridian/Brian Morgan**, 23, 92; **Gallo Images/Hulton Getty**, 33; **Michael Gedye**, 18 (right), 70, 73, 101, 138, 157 (right); **Henebry**, 156; **Hobbs Golf Collection/ Michael Hobbs**, 11, 20 (bottom left), 30, 96, 101, 152, 153; **Eric Hepworth**, 40, 48–49; **Grant Leversha**, 2–3, 126, 142, 144 (bottom), 149, 139; **Brian D Morgan Golf Photography**, 10, 24, 44 (bottom), 45, 46–47, 53, 58–59, 62–63, 80 (right), 87, 88; 90, 93, 114 (bottom), 116, 117, 150–151; **courtesy of Gary Player Design Group**, 56, 57, 72 (left), 81, 82, 94, 95, 124, 125, 154, 155 (left, right); **Kevin Saunders**, 8, 60, 61; **Evan Schiller**, 54, 99, 132; **The Scottish Golf Photo Library/David J Whyte**, 1, 12–13, 15, 20–21 (top), 25, 26, 28, 29, 32, 35, 36 (left), 39, 42 (top right), 118, 121, 122–123; **Phil Sheldon Golf Picture Library**, 38, 42 (top left), 51, 52, 79, 80 (left), 89, 105, 108–109, 136 (top); **Phil Sheldon/Richard J Castka**, 67, 76, 77, 141 (top, bottom); **St Andrews University Library**, 18 (left); **courtesy Sun International**, 145, 146–147; **Tom Treick**, 4–5, 134, 137; **T/A**, 36 (right); **T/A (UK)**, 91; **T/A/Claus Andersen**, 69, 98; **T/A/Simon Bruty**, 55; **T/A/David Cannon**, 6–7, 27 (top), 31, 37, 50, 68, 72 (right), 83, 84, 85, 100, 128, 130, 131, 133, 136 (bottom); **T/A/Duif du Toit**, 148; **T/A/Craig Jones**, 103, 144 (top), **T/A/Tim Matthews**, 115; **T/A/Stephen Munday**, 27 (bottom), 113, 114 (top), 120, 129; **T/A/Gary Newkirk**, 104; **T/A/Tertius Pickard**, endpapers, 127; **T/A/Andrew Redington**, 14; **T/A/Paul Severn**, 16, 110 (right); **T/A/Fred Vuich**, 106, 107.